Contents

Across the Crossfire
was first published in India in 2013 by
Women Unlimited
(an associate of Kali for Women)
K-36, Hauz Khas Enclave
New Delhi 110 016
www.womenunlimited.net

ISBN: 978-81-88965-20-5

Cover design: Neelima Rao
Cover photo: Soma Mitra

Typeset at Sanchauli Image Composer, B-28, Nawada Extension,
Uttam Nagar, New Delhi 110 059
Printed at Chaman Offset, Delhi 110 002

Across the Crossfire

Women and Conflict in India

Edited by
Pamela Philipose & Aditi Bishnoi

women UNLIMITED
an associate of
kali for women

Pamela Philipose is a senior, award-winning journalist who has worked in mainstream newspapers like *The Times of India* and *The Indian Express*. She is presently Director and Editor-in-Chief, Women's Feature Service, a news and feature service that focuses on development and is mandated to visibilise gender in media coverage.

Aditi Bishnoi is Associate Editor, Women's Feature Service. She has a background in communications and has written extensively on issues of social concern.

Women's Feature Service (WFS) is an international not-for-profit media organisation specialising in gender and development issues (www.wfsnews.org). It produces over 300 articles for the media annually, building awareness about women's lives, rights and concerns. Recognising that public policy is made by individuals and institutions, in and outside governments, WFS also makes its work available to varied audiences. In addition, it partners national and international agencies to highlight issues of current concern.

Preface

History has demonstrated, time and again, that women – even though they may not be combatants themselves – have had to bear in large measure the grievous impacts of conflict and violence. These could range from injury and the loss of close family members to dispossession, displacement, and the vulnerabilities and responsibilities that accompany such conditions.

It is in response to this tragic history that International Humanitarian Law (IHL) envisaged general protections for both women and men caught in situations of armed and other forms of conflict. In general, IHL makes mandatory the humane treatment of the wounded and sick, prisoners and civilians. It outlaws hostage-taking and the use of human shields, and lays down that women must especially be protected from sexual violence or the threat of the use of such violence. Additionally, it recognises the right of families to know the fate of missing relatives.

Since conflict often means the absolute destruction of the foundations on which normal life functions – the destruction of homes, the disruption of food and water supplies, and the denial of access to education and health care – IHL makes it obligatory on parties to the conflict to allow the quick and uninterrupted flow of humanitarian relief to those in need of such help. And although IHL aims at preventing and alleviating human suffering in any conflict without discrimination based on gender, it does recognise that women face specific problems in such situations that require comprehensive redressal.

One of the challenges in achieving this, however, lies in the general lack of awareness about the often disproportionate costs that women bear during such crises. Not enough information about women's specific problems during wars, riots or instances of civil unrest has emerged in the public arena, either within the media or in the corridors of power and policy-making. We believe that this book will contribute towards changing social attitudes and refining official interventions, so that women come to be perceived not just as victims of conflict but as part of the process of ushering in recovery and justice in a post-conflict world.

We are grateful to the International Committee of the Red Cross (ICRC) for supporting this project. We wish to clarify that the features in this compilation present the views of their respective writers and do not necessarily reflect in any way the opinions of the publishers or editors.

WOMEN'S FEATURE SERVICE
New Delhi, 2012

Introduction

Let us begin with an intriguing irony. While the impact of conflict and violence on the lives of women in India is well recognised as being deeply destabilising and profoundly disempowering, women for the most part are missing in the conflict discourse. Media reporting on wars, insurgencies, riots, and natural calamities routinely overlooks them; administrative responses to the social disruptions caused by conflict remain insensitive to their special needs; legal regimes and the redress they offer continue to be gender blind; and women remain seriously under-represented at the policy-making and peace-keeping table in the aftermath of situations of conflict. In other words, it is in their absence that women register their presence in the annals of our disturbed times.

It is against this backdrop that we would like to place the present collection of narratives from various zones of conflict in India. Written between 2009 and 2011, these reports focus on the discrete experiences of women caught in insurgencies, wars, riots, situations of civil disorder, and natural calamities in "one of the most culturally diverse and socially fragmented agrarian societies in the world", as political scientist Paul Brass has described India.

The word 'conflict' itself is a multilayered one. Broadly defined as incompatibility between two or more actors that cannot be simultaneously resolved, conflict can range from overt clashes to covert ones; it can entail individual traumas or the collective tensions of an entire community; it could have a verbal dimension or a physical one – and sometimes it could have both; it can exist in popular perception in terms of potentially destablising threats or it can be reflected in concrete and continuing states of armed assault and violence.

International Humanitarian Law recognises two broad categories of armed conflict: international armed conflicts involving two or more States; and non-international armed conflicts between governmental forces and non-governmental groups or between non-governmental groups. The conflicts that this collection documents constitute a spectrum of disruptive developments, violence, struggles, and pitched battles, all of which have resulted in considerable human suffering.

Our intention in putting together this collection is twofold. First, these narratives attempt nothing more ambitious than to tell the stories of women in conflict-ridden regions and situations, women whose voices would not otherwise figure in the public sphere. These are women whose only fault was that they were at the wrong place at the wrong time, caught in a scenario they did not create and over which they had no control. Second, this reportage seeks to explore the commonalities in the experiences of women working in such zones of combat, in different locations and circumstances.

The fact is that conflict plays out in physical/geographical spaces, on people's bodies, as well as in their minds. As living landscapes get radically altered by social tensions, women and girls are disproportionately affected because of their gender. When health centres are rendered non-functional, more women die in childbirth; when neighbourhood schools are converted into police barracks, fewer girls go to school. The loss of income and livelihood generation is immediate and telling. Women who had earlier been earning independent incomes from farming and cattle-rearing are suddenly forced to inhabit relief camps and subsist on doles or forage for forest produce to keep families going. Once the fabric of normal life is destroyed, women also become extremely vulnerable to sexual violence, and coping with the ensuing stigma and social rejection only compounds their existing trauma.

What also comes through with great clarity in this collection is that long after the hostilities have ended – and some could have stretched on for decades – there is a continuing and persistent lack of human security that threatens the well-being of not just the present generation, but that of the future as well. However, the reportage here stands as testimony to the fact that while women may be the victims of enormous violence and conflict, they are also great survivors who display courage, wisdom, and initiative in the most daunting of circumstances. The book's three sections reflect this fact: the first, *Lives, Interrupted*, presents stories of women who have experienced conflict, violence, and calamity at firsthand; the next, *Survival Guides*, is about how the conflict-affected organised themselves to resist repression, deliver education and health care, ensure justice delivery, and rebuild lives, with varying results; the final section, *The Power of One*, focuses on unsung 'she-roes' who have made all the difference in the conflict zone by exerting individual agency.

Health Care: Missing in Action

The long term impact of conflict has many dimensions. Seeds sown a long while ago continue to sprout destruction, as seen in the mined fields of Punjab on the India-Pakistan border. *Farming amidst Landmines: Amputated Lives in Fazilka*, the report that opens the first section of this book, deals with how the landmines laid by the Indian army during Operation Parakram in 2002 still leave the predominantly farming community of Punjab's Fazilka district extremely vulnerable to severely debilitating injuries, the real costs of which are hardly covered by the monetary compensation awarded by the government.

Access to health care in conflict zones is a challenge not just for the poor farmers of Fazilka, but also for those who inhabit the insurgency-hit districts of Odisha like Malkangiri and Nabarangpur. Health care delivery is generally poor in rural India, but the problem is compounded several times over in areas of insurgency. Trained doctors and nurses are unlikely to serve in such regions fearing attack, and regular strike calls by militant groups can mean the crippling of public transport services, leaving the seriously ill in distant villages with no recourse to medical assistance. Two features, *Desperately Seeking Doctors in Odisha's Red Zone* and *Ghost Health Centres to Treat Real People*, deal with these realities, while another, *When Sikkim Shook*, looks at the chaotic emergency health care conditions that prevailed in the small Himalayan state after it suffered an earthquake measuring 6.9 on the Richter scale in September 2011. Whether in Odisha or Sikkim, expectant mothers were the most vulnerable: there are few emergency support services for childbirth in rural India, especially in situations of social chaos. This is one reason why the country reports one of the highest levels of maternal mortality in the world.

It's a similar story when it comes to bomb blasts, even in a metropolis like Mumbai which boasts world-class medical institutions and which has been the site of innumerable blasts and attacks over the last two decades. Doctors interviewed for *Mumbai Blasts: Emergency Response Lost in Transportation* revealed how poor the facilities were in terms of reaching blast victims to hospitals and how limited the infrastructure for emergency medicine in public hospitals.

Life Behind Bars

Conflict and incarceration go hand-in-hand. The uncertain lives, lack of financial support, and the legal battles of women whose husbands are in jail as political prisoners or for trade union activity is addressed in *Conviction and Courage Keep Wives of Political Prisoners Going* and *Arrested Lives: When Trade Union Struggles Came Home.* Visiting the other side of the criminal justice divide, *Behind Police Lines: Edgy Lives of Constables' Wives* looks at the personal lives of the lowly constables – considered the main actors in cases of police brutality and custodial deaths – and concludes that the poor living and service conditions of the police force could be an important contributory factor for the high levels of police atrocities in the country.

The parental rights of women who find themselves in prison, whether for domestic altercations or for crimes, have never been considered an urgent area of reform, although the right to care for one's children is a human right. Going by the experiences of women prisoners documented in *Barred from Life: Experiences of Women Prisoners* and *From the Streets to Jail: Painful Transitions,* the source of greatest agony for women prisoners is the lack of access to their children. As one woman sadly observes, the reason that she stole and was sent to jail was that she needed extra money for her children who are now lost to her.

For some women, life itself has proved to be a jail term. In *Behmai's Widows: "We've Been Left to Die Forever"*, the women whose husbands were gunned down by the woman bandit Phoolan Devi in 1981, exist on the margins of society without any hope of redress. Tragic indeed is the story of Munni Devi, a child bride, who had not even begun to live with her fourteen-year-old husband. She caught her first glimpse of him as a corpse after the massacre and has since had to live the life of a widow in conditions of great privation.

Degrees of Vulnerability

Neither Dantewada nor Lalgarh would have made national news had they not been embroiled in some of the worst conflict-related violence in recent times. Both places – the former in Chhattisgarh and the latter in West Bengal – were sites of Maoist insurgency, with Dantewada continuing to remain so to this day. The Lalgarh conflict saw an unprecedented mobilisation of women, with many espousing the Maoist cause and picking up weapons to form armies of the dispossessed. In *When Women Take Up Arms*, the writer poses the question: how were ordinary women driven to threaten violence against the State? Ultimately, this conflict was about the discontent of a troubled agrarian community fighting for survival in an increasingly rapacious economic and political environment. *How Lalgarh's Flames Engulfed Ordinary Lives* looks at how the Lalgarh conflict came to divide local neighbourhoods right down the middle, with each side left as terrorised and dispossessed as the other.

Violations against children are among the most egregious of crimes committed in situations of conflict. The children of Dantewada have seen close family members being targeted by both Maoist insurgents and the state's security forces. They themselves have been recruited as child soldiers or used as human shields. With their neighbourhoods turned into battlefields, these children have had their homes destroyed and their education disrupted. In *Chhattisgarh's Children, Nobody's Children,* the tragedy of a lost generation is delineated. Meanwhile, as *Life in Salabila: No Relief from Relief Camps* illustrates, the child inhabitants of relief camps in places like Assam's Bongaigaon district grow up to become displaced people without any home to call their own. *The Lost Daughters of Bengal's Border Communities* relates the story of childhoods stolen through rape and abduction: child traffickers, taking advantage of the disturbed, violence-prone circumstances of families living near the Indo-Bangladesh border, spirit away young girls into prostitution.

Rising amidst the Ruins

It is important not to confuse 'powerlessness' with lack of resilience. Time and again, female protagonists in this volume have found themselves without the power to change their realities. However, once they were presented with such an opportunity, they seized it with alacrity and went on to effect some remarkable transformations, as we see in *In the Valley, Women Paramedics with a Healing Touch.* If ensuring education is central to any conflict resolution paradigm, so also is health care delivery. The lack of qualified medical personnel in the conflict-ridden Kashmir of the 1990s led to an interesting experiment: women were recruited from local communities and trained as paramedics. Under the shadow of militancy, these women went on to deliver invaluable medical assistance to ordinary people and, in so doing, also reached out to those suffering from severe psychiatric distress caused by the violence raging around them.

Similarly, *Health Care Workers Deliver Hope in Maoist Country* illustrates what a major difference the Accredited Social Health Activists (ASHAs) have made in the insurgency-hit districts of Odisha that otherwise had no health care worth the name. Like the Kashmiri paramedics, ASHAs are recruited locally and have helped, healed, and saved lives in forgotten swathes of the eastern Indian state. Neighbouring West Bengal also witnessed an audacious experiment when villagers ran makeshift health centres in the Salboni block of the backward Paschim Medinipur district at a point when the state government's health care system had all but collapsed in the face of raging gun battles between security forces and the Maoists. *Delivering Health Care at Gunpoint in Salboni* captures this and also shows how a breakdown in health care delivery can be an important trigger for civil unrest.

Given its long history of conflict, the Northeast has developed many models of peace-building and interventions to resist repression. The Meira Paibis of Manipur are well-known. This group of elderly women made national news in 2001 when they stripped themselves naked to protest an incident of rape and murder by the state's security forces. In *Illness and Debility Can't Stop Manipur's Meira Paibis,* we catch up with these women who, although now considerably older, are still continuing their activism, which is especially focused on preventing violence against women by both local armed groups and the security forces. In other locations in the Northeast – such as Assam's Karbi Anglong Hills district (*High Up in Assam's Hills, a Band of Peace-Builders*) and Manipur's Churachandpur district (*Fighting for Gender Rights in Manipur's Centre of Violence*) – courageous and committed women activists are speaking out and taking action against all forms of violence that women in these areas routinely face, even as they counsel them in the ways of survival.

It is also important not to confuse powerlessness with the lack of hope. Take the young schoolgirls of Govind High School (*6,300 ft above Sea Level, a Kashmir School Helps Girls Reach for the Sky*). Coming from communities marooned by conflict in Jammu and Kashmir's Rajouri district, they trek uncomplainingly for hours to reach their school. Talk to them about what they want to be when they grow up and they will reveal professional ambitions like any schoolchild. But in a region like Kashmir, caught in the vice-like grip of a six-decade-long civil war, their words are portents of better times.

Combating Hate

Communal pogroms in India have undermined the country's secular principles and unleashed trauma, fear, and uncertainty in large sections of society. But many women, despite their lack of literacy and financial stability, have successfully overcome the legacies of hatred created by such tragic episodes. *After the Delhi Riots, How Women Rebuilt their Lives* follows the lives of women who had to flee their childhood homes and neighbourhoods to save themselves and their families when anti-Sikh riots broke out in Delhi in 1984 after the assassination of then-prime minister, Indira Gandhi. It took them decades to regain some control over their circumstances, but they succeeded in doing so without allowing bitterness or despair to destroy them even though justice has never been delivered to them.

How can a state like Gujarat ensure that the terrible anti-Muslim pogrom of 2002 is never repeated? One possible way is outlined in *Lessons from Gujarat: To Prevent Riots, Talk to Children*, which describes how girls and boys from all communities attending government schools were systematically exposed to the idea of a syncretic India in accessible, fun-filled ways. In Odisha, too, interesting peace-building interventions were made in the wake of the anti-Christian attacks of 2007-2008 – and it was women who anchored them, as revealed in *Kandhamal's Wonder Women Fight Hate*.

Conciliation after violence can come about in many ways. It can, for instance, come through personal writing, as *Assam's Women Writers Capture Conflict's Many Shades* indicates; or it could come through getting immersed, once again, in activities that had earlier provided an identity and income, as *Hope among the Ruins: Fulara Wants to Farm Again* shows. It could also come through reaching out to others in similar circumstances. After the Indo-Pak Kargil war, two mothers in the Kangra Valley had to face up to the fact that they would never again see their soldier sons who had been killed in action (*Scars of War: Kargil's Blowback in Kangra*). Today, both women have learnt to rise above their personal grief and are counselling army widows and mothers like themselves who have lost their loved ones to the war and civil conflict. And what happens when two young men from the same village get embroiled in a police encounter which leaves one of them dead and the other in prison? In distant Sanjarpur village, in Uttar Pradesh's Azamgarh district, village women are trying to understand the complexities of the law to defend the reputations of their sons and brothers (*Azamgarh's Women Fight Stigma and Stereotypes*).

Search for Justice

The grief of another mother, in Mumbai this time, is also palpable (*Mother Courage: Turning Grief into a Search for Justice)*. Each time she looks out of the window of her small home in an alley in the heart of that city, Akhtar Hasan Wagle remembers how her seventeen-year-old son was gunned down at that very spot by the police, during the height of the communal tension that engulfed the metropolis in 1993. Today, all these years later, all she wants is that the killers of her innocent son be brought to justice. Nasreen Bano is also a Mumbai riot survivor. The conflagration of 1993 pushed her out of her home and she is fighting for a foothold in the city by arguing for her right to a roof over her head (*A House for Nasreen, Riot-Affected*).

Fifteen years after the 1993 riots, another Mumbai woman watched her husband meet his death live on her television screen. A devastated Kavita Karkare, widow of Hemant Karkare, chief of the Anti-Terrorist Squad, who was killed during the terror attacks on the city on the night of November 26, 2008, is now publicly demanding better protection for those on the frontlines of policing, as well as a more transparent police administration (*Kavita Karkare's Courage Quotient*).

All these women are unlikely crusaders. Personal circumstances forced them to articulate the larger concerns that are embedded in situations of violence. Their diligent assertions have had far-reaching impact. Rafat Seema, a teacher by profession, could have opted for a life of academic pursuits, but instead she chose to assist the families of men jailed after the Mecca Masjid blasts that rocked Hyderabad in 2007, many of whom were later released for lack of evidence. She did this despite being told by well-wishers that she would only be inviting trouble by getting involved. But, as she points out in *Fighting for Prisoners' Rights, Clad in a Burqa*, the basic rights of women and children related to these incarcerated men were being violated and she felt she had to help them at a point when they were being shunned by most others and branded the family members of 'terrorists'.

Unsung Saviours

Not just articulate urban women, but rural women like Prabhavati, working in an anganwadi in Bihar's disturbed Jehanabad district, have made difficult choices too. She rejected the path of violence that her husband, a Maoist leader, had chosen for himself, arguing that she contributed more effectively to society by educating village children rather than by waging war against the State (*Maoist Violence is not Prabhavati's Way*). The response of Asma Khan to the communal frenzy of Gujarat was similar. She reached out to children orphaned by the 2002 pogrom, taking care to inculcate in them the values of humanity and respect for others (*Gujarat Riot Kids Come Home – To Faraway Delhi*). Another school teacher, this time in Assam's Sharon village, made sure that the education of her students did not suffer even after their school building and homes had been burnt down during fierce clashes between the Dimasas and Hmars in 2003 (*There's No Stopping Bimala's School*). How did Bimala achieve this? By turning her own home, which had fortunately escaped the conflagration, into a school for local children. Regular classes were held and examinations conducted on schedule in these most extraordinary circumstances!

Ultimately, it comes down to life choices. Gynaecologist Dr. Rani Bang, trained at the prestigious Johns Hopkins University School of Medicine, could have practiced her profession anywhere in the country, in comfort and amidst great wealth (*In Gadchiroli's Zone of Fear, a Doctor Saves Lives*). Instead, she took the road less travelled, putting her powers of healing at the service of some of India's poorest communities: the tribals of conflict-scarred Gadchiroli district of Maharashtra. Finally, there is C. Thenmozhi, a Tamil refugee who has proved a refuge to many who, like her, were compelled to flee Sri Lanka's civil war and make their way to Tamil Nadu, leaving behind their homes and dreams (*A Sri Lankan Tamil Refugee Builds New Worlds*). When asked why she did this, she smiled and said, "Someone had to do it."

Many Voices, Many Concerns

When taken together, the stories in this volume raise many issues and argue for urgent changes – in the law, in the administration, and in the way the country considers such issues. Human rights advocates have long campaigned for the idea of reparations to become part of Indian jurisprudence. Reparations go far beyond mere relief and rehabilitation interventions; they also include concepts like the restitution of rights and the guarantee of non-recurrence of acts of violence and repression.

Internally Displaced Persons also need to be recognised as a category of people entitled to a specific protection regime. Far too many men, women, and children are wasting their lives away in derelict relief camps in many corners of the country without any hope of leading lives as equal citizens.

These stories also testify to the principle that no matter the situation, no matter the severity of conflict, two rights are non-negotiable: people's right to health care and children's right to education. Lack of health care has emerged as one of the most serious challenges in situations of conflict – precisely where it is needed the most. It is time to seriously consider putting in place alternative systems of health care in affected regions. The role played by ASHAs in assisting critically ill women in insurgency-affected districts of Odisha or by the paramedical teams of Jammu and Kashmir in delivering health care to the doorstep are, despite their inadequacies, good examples of such alternative health regimes.

Sexual violence perpetrated by State and non-State actors in situations of conflict is widespread, but continues to be under-reported and poorly addressed because of the social stigma it entails. Thus, affected women are dealt a double injury: first at the hands of their rapists, and then by their families and community. The criminal justice system has become so cynical in such cases that heinous acts are dismissed as routine or perceived as being part of collateral damage. More often than not, it needs the involvement of local women activists for a modicum of justice to come the way of assaulted women.

In fact, many crimes against women in zones of conflict do not even have a legal language to define them – so how can they begin to get addressed? This is why it is so important that the stories in this volume are heard – not just in the areas where such crimes have played out, but in the country as a whole.

Finally, if there is a single insight that emerges from these pages, it is this: women who have found themselves on the frontlines of violence have invariably risen to the challenge the situation poses. They have found ways to cope with every reversal while actively evolving methods to respond to the crises around them. Clearly, their presence as central players in formal conflict-resolution and peace-keeping forums is critical for a durable and just peace. Their wisdom and experiences must shape the lifelines to the future.

As Maya Angelou observed, "History, despite its wrenching pain, cannot be unlived, but if faced with courage, need not be lived again."

PAMELA PHILIPOSE

Lives, Interrupted

"I had gone to fetch fodder... when my right foot slipped and I stepped on a landmine."

Farming amidst Landmines: Amputated Lives in Fazilka

Tripti Nath

Fazilka (Punjab): The rural folk of Fazilka, a subdivision in Punjab, have often had to pay a heavy price for living in perilous proximity to the India-Pakistan border. Many have lost their lives to the innumerable landmines laid by the Indian army during Operation Parakram, along the international border in Jammu and Kashmir, Rajasthan, and Punjab, following the terrorist attack on the Indian Parliament in December 2001. The mines are said to have been laid at a density of 1,000 per square kilometre.

The stories of villagers 'lucky' enough to have survived these landmines are heart-rending. Take Raj Kaur, 55, an inhabitant of village Bhamba Wattu, which lies just six kilometres from the international border. Nine years ago, she inadvertently stepped on a landmine while walking along a narrow mud track leading to her village. By the time she could fathom what had gone wrong, she had stepped on another landmine. Ever since that day, Raj has lead an agonising existence: she has lost both her legs below the knees. The woman who once earned a living as an agricultural worker has been forced to sit all day on her string cot, guarding her lifelines: her prosthetic aids and walker.

Every detail of that tragic day that changed her life is etched in her mind. She remembers how her husband, Balbir Singh, rushed her to the civil hospital in Jalalabad, thirty-three kilometres away. The authorities there administered first aid and referred the couple to the army hospital at the district headquarters of Ferozepur, some eighty-five kilometres away. There she received prosthetic aids that served her for some time. Only in February 2008 did she succeed in getting proper prosthetic devices at a camp supported by civil society organisations.

While the family received financial assistance from the government, it was not adequate. The compensation that Balbir Singh managed to secure after running from pillar to post was just Rs 1,50,000. Using the interest-free loan of Rs 10,000 granted by the Delhi-based Rajiv Gandhi Foundation, the couple was able to help their younger son, Jaswant, open a barber's shop. Raj bemoaned her fate: "We have no land. I was earning almost Rs 4,000 a month as an agricultural worker, but the accident has left me incapacitated."

Another landless labourer, Surjeet Kaur, of village Behak Khas, located around eight kilometres from the border, has been coping with disability for over a decade. "I had gone to fetch fodder for the livestock when my right foot slipped and I stepped on a landmine. All that is left of the foot is the heel," she said.

Surjeet was already disabled even before the fateful landmine accident: one of the toes of her left foot had been amputated as a result of a snake bite when she was six. "I had learnt to manage with an amputated toe, but it is difficult to manage without one half of the foot. The army helped me get a prosthetic aid from Chandigarh (capital of the states of Punjab and Haryana), but over time it has lost its utility," she said. In these times of rising costs, keeping the family going has been a challenge for Surjeet, who has three daughters and a son. The government compensation of Rs 1,50,000 that came her way was spent on a daughter's marriage.

Struggling to make ends meet, Surjeet's husband, Harbans Singh, moves from village to village in search of agricultural work as a daily wage labourer. Surjeet, too, despite her disability, goes in search of wage work to Kheo Wali Dhab – fifteen kilometres from her home – leaving her children in the care of her mother-in-law.

Why didn't Surjeet take the time out to get a proper prosthetic? "The choice was between two square meals a day or a prosthetic. Before the landmine accident, I was working as an agricultural labourer and that is all I can do," answered the victim matter-of-factly, as she revealed that even travelling to the prosthetic centre in Chandigarh was an expensive proposition for her.

A mere two kilometres from the Indo-Pak border, in Jhangal Baini village, Mitoo Bai, 35, lives with her pre-teen children. Mitoo was in her twenties when she lost her right foot after stepping on a landmine while in the fields gathering fodder for the family cattle. Since the accident, she has been hobbling around the house with the help of a walking stick. While she has had prosthetic boots made twice over, she felt they were not very useful. "Now I wear canvas shoes and walk with great difficulty. When my foot hurts a lot, I take painkillers," she said.

Like the other women, Mitoo has been struggling to make ends meet. "We got Rs 1,50,000 from the Centre, but that is not enough compensation for a disability that is life-long. Should the state government not be sensitive to our condition?" she asked.

A source in the army pointed out that the Ministry of Defence gives ex gratia compensation to all civilian victims of landmines: "The policy has been in place since January 2003. The army gives Rs 2,50,000 to next of kin in cases of casualty, Rs 2,00,000 in cases of 100 per cent disability, Rs 1,50,000 in cases of disability assessed between 50 to 100 per cent, and Rs 1,00,000 in cases where disability is below 50 per cent." But the officer admitted that the paperwork involved was very exhaustive.

Of course, the army disagreed with the victims' grievance that it hasn't cared to follow up on prostheses. Explained another officer, "No patient came back to us. If they approach us, follow-up action will be taken. If we had gone all the way to get prostheses fitted, nothing really holds us back from organising a follow-up. At that time, funds for the expense incurred on transportation, accommodation, diet, treatment, including the cost of prostheses, was provided by the Service concerned. Artificial limb centres in Chandigarh, Bhavnagar, Jaipur, and Ludhiana, were also supported by the army for the provision of prostheses."

The army also rejected criticism that warning markers on several acres of land along the India-Pakistan border were either missing or not legible. One officer put it this way: "During Operation Parakram, the army had laid landmines which were in consonance with well-practiced, relevant, and standard operating procedures, including physical verification of the mines and a meticulous drill during laying out these mines. Special emphasis had been laid on the recording and marking of each minefield to prevent civilian casualties."

Sources also claimed that the army had made all efforts to ensure the safety of civilians. Caution notices were put up in all border villages by the state and district administrations and the local police was informed about the presence of the minefields. There was also prominent perimeter fencing with barbed wires and conspicuous marking and warning signs, in both English and the local language, at close intervals, to indicate the presence of minefields and alert civilians.

According to the army, almost the entire area was, in any case, de-mined after Operation Parakram. Yet, while sources did concede that mines could drift due to the melting of the snows or sub-soil erosion, they hastened to add that whenever such developments are brought to its notice, the army takes prompt action, in addition to taking pre-emptive steps like conducting regular monitoring exercises.

The residents of the vulnerable villages, however, have continued to live in fear of the hidden dangers that lurk in their fields and pathways. Many among them have already been struggling for years with the consequences of having stepped on a stray landmine that has led either to death or a family member becoming permanently disabled.

This is a region known for the high value of its fertile agricultural land, but for some that very land has turned out to be the source of a lifetime of pain and suffering.

Chhattisgarh's Children, Nobody's Children

Manipadma Jena

Raipur (Chhattisgarh): A traumatised Sunita Hemla, 13, has relived every moment of her father's last hours a thousand times over. It was the dead of night when seven masked men visited her parents' home in Santoshpur village of Bijapur district in Chhattisgarh. The strangers revealed themselves to be Maoists and demanded that Sunita's father step out or else they would kill the young girl and her two siblings. Fearing for his children's lives, Sunita's father, Masa Ram, gave himself up. At dawn, his battered body was found in the backyard of the family home.

Sunita is not the only young witness to such terror. Sarita Netam, 14, another local girl, lost her father, Ganapat, under eerily similar circumstances. Ganapat, the headman of the Ambelli gram panchayat, also in Bijapur district, was killed because he would not hand over to the local militants the twenty-four boys and girls they were demanding for induction into their cadres. Revealed Sarita, "Two days after they took him, my elder aunt who lived in the neighbouring village found his body in her millet field. His limbs had been tied together and his body bore multiple hatchet wounds. He had been repeatedly dunked in the village pond with the objective of extracting information, and then left to die." Every detail of this tragic story seemed seared into the mind of the young girl as she narrated it.

Since 2004, Chhattisgarh has been one of the states worst hit by the Maoist insurgency. According to data from the Union Ministry of Home Affairs, 1,483 people were killed between 2004 and 2008 in such violence, with civilians accounting for 828 of the deaths. We visited the worst-affected districts of Dantewada and Bijapur in 2009 to understand the impact of the violence, especially on children.

The situation in Dantewada was grave. The district had

been locked in a civil war-like situation since 2005, with Maoist insurgents pitted against the security forces in a brutal stand-off. An armed anti-insurgency squad known as the Salwa Judum – which, ironically, means 'a movement to restore peace' – was set up in 2005 to counter Maoist violence, but ended up replicating and perpetuating it. Members of the Salwa Judum would visit villages, hold pre-announced meetings, exhort local tribals to resist the Maoists, and then proceed to capture alleged militants who often ended up being killed. There were many occasions when the Salwa Judum would run amok, burning down the houses of known or suspected insurgents in the region.

The resultant atmosphere of conflict and uncertainty had forced local tribal communities to flee the area even if this meant deserting their ancestral homes and villages. They would either end up in government relief camps or migrate to the bordering districts of Andhra Pradesh or simply disappear into the forests seeking the protection of the insurgents.

Over the years, thousands of children were caught in this scenario of violence and uncertainty. In many cases, they had to fend for themselves, not knowing whether their parents were dead or alive. The conflict had come home to them in at least three distinct ways. First, many were drawn directly into the vortex of violence. According to local sources, arms – even AK 47s – were sometimes strapped onto the bodies of children, who were then used as human shields by the perpetrators of violence in order to protect themselves. Children would also be used as conduits in the passing of secret information or be made to plant bombs and landmines.

Moreover, numerous youngsters were made to engage directly in armed hostilities, including the teenagers who signed up for the Chhattisgarh Police Service as special police officers. Recruited for a salary of Rs 3,000, under Section 17 of the Police Act, 1861 and Section 9 of the Chhattisgarh Police Act, 2000, they would find themselves at the frontlines of the offensive against the insurgents after having been trained to deploy the most brutal means of violence themselves. It was only in mid-2011 that the Supreme Court of India intervened to stop such recruitment.

Of course, this conflict resulted in the loss of basic schooling for Chhattisgarh's children – the second big impact of violence on them. According to a Human Rights Watch report, *Dangerous Duty* (September 2008), around 40 per cent of children between the ages of six and sixteen, who had been residing in government-sponsored rehabilitation camps in Chhattisgarh, had not been attending school. In order to prevent local tribals from joining the ranks of the Maoists, the state government had opened twenty-three makeshift relief camps in Dantewada and Bijapur, many of them located in local schools. Not surprisingly then, according to one estimate, since 2005, no less than 260 schools in abandoned villages in the two districts had either been relocated or shut down.

The National Human Rights Commission, in its 2008 inquiry report, conducted in response to writ petitions alleging excesses by security forces and Salwa Judum cadres, also noted that both occupied school buildings for months. Since these schools were used as operational bases, they sometimes came under Maoist fire and became the scene of pitched battles, which reduced school infrastructure to rubble in some areas.

International Humanitarian Law prohibits the destruction of schools – which are regarded as civilian objects – unless such buildings are occupied by the military. The National Commission for Protection of Child Rights also recommends that schools be recognised by all parties to a conflict as "zones of peace". But these recommendations were clearly overlooked by the state as evidenced by the very poor literacy figures at the time: Dantewada had a literacy rate of 20.5 per cent for women and 39.5 per cent for men, compared to the state average of 65.18 per cent (Census 2001).

The third significant impact observed on children's lives was the dislocation brought on by a conflict that had torn apart the very fabric of family life. Kamli Hapka's was one such family. Kamli, 37, lost her husband, Mangu, the sarpanch (village head) of Ghumra in Bijapur, to the insurgency. Then her son was lost to her because he was recruited into the Salwa Judum and she didn't hear of him after that. Her daughter, Aarti, 12, had to be sent away to a kanya ashram (a residential school for girls, run by the Chhattisgarh government) in Dhanora. The ashram was later set on fire and Aarti had to be relocated to a shelter for children affected by conflict in Raipur, the state capital. Although she was safe, Aarti was about 500 kilometres away from her family members and could not contact them even in an emergency.

Aarti, Sunita, and Sarita, along with twenty-six other girls, were all housed in the Raipur shelter. When we met them, they smiled hesitantly for the camera, but their faces bore evidence of the deep trauma that had marked their young lives. These were children who never got the chance to live their childhood and were soon to be young adults without a future. All because of a conflict they had no role in creating.

After the Garo-Rabha Clashes, Malaria and Hunger

Ratna Bharali Talukdar

Kukurkata (Assam): A bumper crop during the agriculture season, the birth of a baby boy one month ahead of Magh Bihu – the harvest festival that falls in mid-January – and her husband's promise to buy a two-wheeler with his increased income as a small trader in the East Garo Hills district of Meghalaya, were reasons enough to make Himani Rabha, 27, smile.

This Rabha tribal woman from Teklipara I village, located in the Goalpara district of Assam that lies close to the Assam-Meghayala border, could never have imagined that a totally unexpected conflict would turn her world upside down, that she would have to flee her home and live in sub-human conditions in a makeshift relief camp at Kukurkata in Assam.

Inter-tribal clashes broke out between the Garos and Rabhas in the first week of January 2011 and the violence and arson that followed displaced 60,000 people in both Assam and Meghalaya. The two tribes, which had peacefully coexisted since the days of their ancestors, were locked in a stand-off that may not have claimed many lives – twelve casualties were reported – but which rendered thousands homeless. Over 40,000 people took refuge in the thirty-odd relief camps that came up across Assam, while ten camps set up in Meghalaya became the temporary homes of nearly 20,000 others.

Life for Himani and other Rabha women in the Kukurkata camp was fraught with hunger, poverty, and panic. Food was hard to come by: most of the displaced people couldn't afford even one square meal a day. And since provisions for health care were almost non-existent, pregnant women were the worst hit. In the name of sanitation, the Public Health and Engineering Department set up pit toilets, but open defecation was common, creating serious health and hygiene concerns.

The education of school-going children was put on hold as most of the village schools close by had been burnt down in the clashes. This disruption of life also meant no jobs. The high level of unemployment gave families sleepless nights because they had no idea how they would ever manage to get back on their feet without financial resources. Conversations with Himani and other women in the Kukurkata camp indicated how tragically disruptive are the ethnic clashes that regularly break out in this region. "Our granaries, full of paddy, and our homes were set ablaze by miscreants. Animals, fowl, and properties were either looted or destroyed. We were left with no means to even resume a normal life. In such a situation, with my jobless husband and three children, we have no idea what to do for survival," said a completely distraught Himani.

Following the violence, unemployment became a major issue. Traditionally, the livelihoods of the Garos and Rabhas has been interlinked: the men from Assam – Garo or Rabha – cross over to Meghalaya to work in the coal mines or in small business ventures there as daily wagers, while Rabha women make dakmandas, the typical dress of Garo women, because the Garos don't have a weaving tradition. However, in the aftermath of the ethnic tensions, this age-old relationship completely broke down.

Things took a turn for the worse when, two months after the clashes, the state discontinued its assistance and with it the flow of relief material and rations for camp inmates also ended. Some external aid helped during this time of deep crisis. Himani, for instance, was able to construct a temporary shed with a tarpaulin sheet provided by the Assam state branch of the Indian Red Cross Society (IRCS) and the International Committee of the Red Cross (ICRC). The lone blanket, also provided by ICRC, was her family's only protection against the cold at night, while her kitchen was lined with cooking utensils given as part of the relief kit: two cooking pots, five bowls, five full plates, five glasses, five cups, five tablespoons, two serving spoons, and one knife. But while the cutlery and crockery were there, food stocks were still low because of limited funds. Himani's five-member family lived on one meal a day in a bid to make the rehabilitation grant of Rs 10,000, that it had received from the Assam government to rebuild the family home, go as far as possible.

Another major challenge that Himani faced due to her changed circumstances was the deteriorating health of her three children. Her newborn baby was not able to get proper attention because the health sub-centre at Kukurkata lacked personnel. And while her two school-going children would have got their government-funded midday meals had they been attending their old school, they were now becoming pale and listless because of poor nourishment.

Almost each one of the Rabha women at the Kukurkata camp had a similar story to relate. They all longed to go back home to their old lives. In fact, some had bravely made their way back to their villages, but quickly returned with horrific stories about how the whole area looked like a war zone. Importantly, they found there was no source of safe drinking water because the existing water sources, mostly wells, had been contaminated by the rioters.

Displacement has always posed specific problems for women that seldom get articulated in policy-making. But talking to the women at Kukurkata provided important glimpses into some of these. Take Triveni Rabha, 30, who was eight months pregnant at the time. Her prematurely lined face bore evidence of the tough experiences she had had to face in her condition. She recalled how her family escaped its burning home and crossed a river before finding safety at the Kukurkata police outpost. Her husband, Dilip, was later compelled to go out in search of work, leaving his pregnant wife behind. She was in dire need of proper rest and food but barely got to eat more than once a day. The one lifeline Triveni had in those difficult days was the local Accredited Social Health Activist (ASHA). "The village ASHA attended to me regularly and tried to give me as much help as possible. She also reassured me by saying that she would be around when it was time for the delivery and that was a big consolation," she said.

The other concern that loomed large during those days was the changing weather. With the onset of the rainy season in June, life only got tougher: refugee tents began to leak and there was slush all around. But what was really worrying was the threat of malaria – in the border areas of north-east India, malaria outbreaks are common. While the Congress-led coalition government in Assam had made budgetary provisions for the distribution of medicated mosquito nets and blankets among the poor, most of these had already been distributed in the first quarter of the year as poll freebies, in anticipation of the Assam assembly elections in April. Predictably, none of the families in Kukurkata got any.

Despite all these difficulties, the Rabha women did not admit defeat. They went about piecing together the shards of their broken lives, bit by bit, drawing heart from their collective strength. Their first move was to request civil society organisations to help them set up looms so that they could resume their weaving to earn some money. The Assam state branch of the IRCS also helped out with a Micro Economic Initiative Programme to enable the women to take on various economic activities based on their traditional skills and aptitude.

It is only through cooperation, not conflict, that the future can be secured – this was the implicit message that the hard-working Rabha women sent out to those who had lit and then fanned the flames of conflict that engulfed the region and their lives.

Desperately Seeking Doctors in Odisha's Red Zone

Sarada Lahangir

Malkangiri (Odisha): A doctor is a rare sight in Malkangiri, one of Odisha's poorest districts and the site of a long-running Maoist insurgency. Yet, if any community needs affordable health care, it is this one, caught as it is between insurgency and chronic malnutrition.

The case of Minati Kirsani, a young woman resident of Petal, a predominantly tribal village in Malkangiri, shines a light on the situation here. When she was seven months pregnant, Minati suddenly developed acute stomach cramps and was taken to the Paplur Primary Health Centre (PHC), around ten kilometres from the village. An ayurvedic doctor, Prassanna Ku Patra, attended to her. He administered a dose of intravenous glucose, but Minati's condition deteriorated rapidly. Finally, her hapless husband, Raghuram, acting on the advice of the doctor, decided to take her to the hospital at Chitrokonda, about forty kilometres from Paplur. Unfortunately, no transport was immediately available, so Raghuram decided to take Minati back home. She did not survive the ordeal.

Patra, the only doctor in these parts, routinely has to handle cases of this kind from the fifteen villages in the area. When we met him to ask about Minati's case, he sounded helpless. "The case was quite complicated. Here, in this new PHC, we have almost no infrastructure. No electricity, no water supply, no ambulance facility. And the general fear of the Maoists has ensured that timely public transport is also not available. I did my best, but unfortunately couldn't save this patient's life," he said.

Tulema Hental of Badpada village, which lies in an inaccessible part of Malkangiri, is another young mother who died in childbirth. When she first went into labour, nobody in her family realised the seriousness of the situation. The baby emerged in the breech position and the young mother began to bleed profusely. The local midwife, Kali Hentalo, tried to salvage the situation, but Tulema's condition soon turned critical. At that late stage, the family tried to take her to a hospital in Chitrokonda. But because of a bandh (shut down) call given by the Maoists, no transportation was available and Tulema passed away.

The stories of Minati and Tulema are not unusual in Malkangiri, where the official Maternal Mortality Rate (MMR) is 30 per 200 live births, according to the office of the chief district medical officer. Out of 14,982 deliveries in the district in 2009-10, only 6,122 took place in a health care institution.

The growing insurgency in Malkangiri has certainly taken a heavy toll on health care delivery systems. While the insurgents have not directly attacked any health establishment or health personnel so far, the frequent road blockades, ambushes on police parties, and threats to government officials in the affected areas have left health care services in complete disarray. In 2011, of the 111 sanctioned posts for doctors in the district, 71 posts were lying vacant; similarly, 50 per cent of paramedical posts remained unfilled and half of the PHCs had no doctors.

Legislators cutting across party lines have admitted that most of the doctors and paramedics emerging from the state-run medical colleges do not wish to work in Malkangiri, despite attractive pay packages and incentives from the state government, due to security concerns. Their fears are not unfounded. This is the same region from where R. Vineel Krishna, the serving district collector, was abducted by Maoists in February 2011, as the country watched in helpless anxiety.

According to Malkangiri's chief district medical officer, C.H. Pravakar, "Women and children here are severely undernourished. Although no formal study has been done, our health workers from villages like Janbai, Jodamba, Badpada, and Jantapai have informed us about the high MMR and the alarming levels of anaemia among the nursing mothers."

Pravakar also said that many maternal deaths remained unreported and that his office was quite helpless in managing the situation: "We are trying our best to deliver good health services, but what can we do? First, the area is almost inaccessible, given the bad roads. Second, bandh calls by the Maoists for at least twenty days in a month ensure that there is no transportation worth the name. So how do we dispatch the medicines and food material under schemes like the Integrated Child Development Services to women who desperately need them?"

Local people talk of having to walk for miles, carrying sick relatives in bamboo baskets or on a cot, in order to get them some medical care in the nearest town. The roads are badly damaged and the Balimela reservoir has ensured that some 151 villages remain completely cut off from the mainland by a large body of water. Earlier, there was a regular launch service to ferry people across the waters, but after the Alampaka incident of 2008 – in which thirty-eight security personnel were killed in a Maoist attack – there is only one service a day. The few boats available take over six hours to traverse the forty to fifty kilometres from the Balimela spillway to the villages on the banks of the reservoir. This leaves villagers living there with no option but to suffer and wait endlessly should they be confronted with a medical emergency.

Visiting the region was an eye-opener. A PHC opened in Badpada in 2005 was still awaiting its first doctor years later at the end of 2011. In the nearby village of Papermelta, Sania Matem, 60, held the slight, feverish form of her two-year-old grandson in her arms. There was fear on her face as she pleaded with anyone she came across for medicines to save the child. Her daughter-in-law had died while giving birth to him; in that case too, her family had not been able to provide the young woman with timely medical attention.

According to Dr. Khirod Chandra Mahanto, a senior doctor at the Chitrokonda Community Health Centre, "Everything comes to a standstill here after 6 p.m. because of the fear of the Naxalites. Earlier, doctors and auxiliary staff would respond to a call from an interior region. Not any more. It's the fear factor that operates here."

An auxiliary nursing midwife from Badpada added, "If a district collector can be abducted here, then what about ordinary people like us? Who will guarantee our safety? We want to work and serve the people, but not at the cost of our lives."

When R. Vineel Krishna, who got transferred from Malkangiri after he was released from captivity, was asked about the problem of health care delivery in the region, he was not keen to say too much on the issue. This was perhaps understandable given his own harrowing experience. But he did say that the district administration in the interior pockets of Malkangiri was very conscious of the problem and was trying hard to improve the situation.

But can Krishna's words of hope be of any consolation to the thousands suffering here? How long will it be before women like the elderly Sania Matem, who was desperately seeking medical attention for her frail and sickly grandson, can access health care without fear?

Ghost Health Centres to Treat Real People

Sarada Lahangir

Nabarangpur (Odisha): It would be wrong to say that there was no health infrastructure in Odisha's tribal-dominated, insurgency-affected Nabarangpur district. In 2011, on paper at least, there were thirty-seven Primary Health Centres (PHCs) and seven Community Health Centres (CHCs) covering the ten blocks in the district.

But impressive as these figures sound, in terms of health delivery on the ground they were hardly making a difference. Here's how alarming the health personnel shortage in Nabarangpur was in 2011: at the district headquarters' hospital, on which more than three lakh people were dependent, there were ten positions lying vacant, including key posts in the departments of medicine, orthopaedics, paediatrics, obstetrics and gynaecology, eye, skin, anaesthesia, pathology, and surgery. The situation in the block areas was no better: at least twenty subdivisional hospitals were being run solely by health workers and nurses, while certain facilities in the very remote areas were being managed by Class Four employees without any real professional medical training. This was the situation at the PHCs: thirty-six posts of surgeons were vacant in 2011 and no doctors had been posted in the eleven specialist departments in the last decade. Moreover, no doctor had ever been posted at PHCs near the villages of Kosagumuda, Papadahandi, Dabugam, Jharigam, Chandahandi, Nandahandi, and Tentulikhunti, while at the seven CHCs in Nabarangpur, posts for senior medical officers had been lying unfilled for the past twelve years.

Despite this grim reality, there seemed to be no urgency on the part of the state machinery to look for a workable solution. This is no real surprise as the authorities in the state capital, Bhubaneswar, usually sat up and took action only when there was the occasional tragedy. In 2004, for instance, the villages of Dongriguda and Jharigam made it to the front pages of the local newspapers when twelve children died due to the lack of timely medical care for illnesses related to malnutrition. At that point, the government promised to improve the health care system at the village level, but once the public outrage died down nothing happened. The deaths were soon forgotten.

How were local people coping with this serious shortfall in health care delivery? According to Kusuma Gauda, 50, a resident of Chandahandi village, "No doctor has been sighted here for years. The Chandahandi PHC is run by a pharmacist. During times when the incidents of malaria and diarrhoea increase, a mobile medical unit does come by. But it is usually around only for a day or so. For the rest of the year, we are dependent on the medicines given by our local village medicine man. We have no other alternative."

Dependence on 'medicine men', or those selling indigenous therapies, seemed to be common in Nabarangpur. These medicine men made quick money because few people here were able to afford to go to the big Berhampur Medical College and Hospital in Ganjam district or to hospitals in Visakhapatnam in the neighbouring state of Andhra Pradesh.

The topography of the region, too, has contributed to the misery. Much of Nabarangpur is hilly and has only fair weather roads. During the monsoons, people have to walk or, at best, ride a cycle. This situation is particularly trying for pregnant women. According to Sushama Jain, an activist who works for the local civil society organisation, Jagruti, "In Nabarangpur, which has one of the highest Infant Mortality Rates (IMR) in Odisha, women nearing their delivery date sometimes have to travel fifty to sixty kilometres to the district hospital through terrain that can be covered only on foot and which could entail crossing rivers. No other modes of transportation exist here."

When Bimala Majhi, 30, of Dongriguda village went into labour, she had to be rushed to the only CHC in the area, located at Jharigam. To reach there, she had to endure a long and arduous journey: she travelled the first ten kilometres to

Badtemra village in a bamboo basket carried by her husband, Dhanapati, and his two nephews. It took them forty-five minutes to cover that distance. From there, she travelled another thirty-six kilometres by bus. By the time she reached the poorly-equipped Jharigam CHC, she had developed severe complications and was referred to the subdivisional hospital at Umerkot, about eleven kilometres away. An autorickshaw was hired, but when the family reached Umerkot they found that the only doctor there was on leave. So Bimala had to be taken to the district headquarters' hospital at Nabarangpur, where she underwent a Caesarean section and gave birth to a baby girl who died a day later.

For any mother, the loss of a child is tragic. But when this scene is replayed around these parts, many times over every day, it does provoke the question: where is the health care for the people who need it most? "Our village is very remote," said a dejected Dhanapati. "Every year, people here are dying because accessing any form of health care is difficult. And even if there is a health centre in the area, it is often of little use because there are no medical personnel in attendance."

As was evident in Bimala's case, only the hospital at the district headquarters was equipped to come to the rescue of critically ill patients; there was simply no one in the PHCs or CHCs to handle emergencies. Sushama Jain revealed that even if these patients did manage to reach the PHC/CHC in time and there was a medical worker in attendance, chances were that nothing would be done. "If the case is complicated, local personnel do not even touch these patients. They are immediately referred to the district hospital," she said.

This delay in attending to the critically ill was responsible for the high number of maternal deaths in the state, especially among tribal women. The figure for deaths of infants below five years, too, was poor: nearly 90 for every 1,000 children, according to the Comptech Tribal Rehabilitation Society, an organisation that did an IMR survey of Nabarangpur. Several tribal women had no choice but to deliver babies in their homes, because family members did not see any benefit in travelling for hours to a congested hospital where there would be no trained doctor to oversee treatment. In 2010-2011, for instance, there was no gynaecologist posted anywhere in the district.

Dr. Manoj Parida, the doctor in charge at the Umerkot zonal hospital in 2011, acknowledged the lack of good doctors and medical support staff that afflicted the region: "Besides a lack of infrastructure, in this hospital, for instance, out of nine posts for doctors, only three – which includes me – are filled. Four posts have been vacant during my entire tenure of six years. We don't even have an anaesthetist here so how can we conduct major operations? Whenever we come across a serious patient we have no option but to refer them to the district headquarters' hospital."

The former chief district medical officer of Nabarangpur, Dr. J.K. Behera, also explained how the entire health system had been brought to its knees here: "This is one of the most backward and underdeveloped tribal districts in Odisha. There is a lack of proper connectivity and good educational facilities. Making matters worse has been the sharp increase in Maoist insurgency in the district and the situation is only getting worse. Fearing for their lives, doctors are unwilling to work in the district."

Ultimately, what good would the empty shell of a PHC or hospital be for people suffering from serious health problems in an insurgency-hit district? The health authorities in Nabarangpur had no answers.

Behmai's Widows: "We've Been Left to Die Forever"

Yogesh Vajpeyi

Kanpur Dehat (Uttar Pradesh): Behmai village was in the news over three decades ago when Phoolan Devi and her gang of dacoits gunned down twenty men here on February 14, 1981. Decades later, there are many in the village who still remember that day, but possibly no one more than Munni Devi. "I feel like something that has been used, abused by the world, and then discarded," she told us when we visited Behmai, which falls in the Kanpur Dehat district of Uttar Pradesh (UP). One of those gunned down on that fateful day was Munni's husband, Lal Singh.

Like most girls in the region, Munni was only thirteen when her parents married her to Lal Singh, a boy from Behmai, all of fourteen himself. Local custom required her to continue living with her parents in Tengua village, situated across the river Yamuna in the adjoining Jalaun district, until her gauna, a second marriage ceremony held some years after the first, after which the groom takes the bride to his home.

The teenaged bride was preparing for her new life when fate intervened. She was still at her parents' home when news came of the now-infamous Behmai massacre in which her husband was also killed. "I had not even seen his face. I only got to see his dead body," she recalled.

A year later, tragedy struck young Munni's life once again – this time she lost her parents. And before she could come to terms with her loss, she had to pack her bags and shift to the home of her in-laws in Behmai.

The helplessness and despair that Munni felt at that point does not seem to have faded with time. In fact, abject poverty and memories of the tragedy have branded her life ever since. "I have nowhere to go. I have no child to support me. I receive no pension from the government. I am at the mercy of God and my husband's family," she wept.

Immediately after the killings, almost the entire state government machinery descended on the scene of the crime in Behmai. Led by the then UP Chief Minister, Vishwanath Pratap Singh, the administration promised jobs to the relatives of the victims and pensions to their widows. Three decades have passed and none of the twelve surviving Behmai widows are receiving support any longer. Only one relative from each victim's family was given a constable's job with the state police.

"We did receive a pension of Rs 25 per month for a couple of years after the massacre, but then it stopped suddenly. We approached district officials in faraway Kanpur city, but ended up spending money over futile journeys without any results," revealed Santoshi Devi, 60, who had helplessly watched her husband, Banwari, plead for his life before being gunned down by Phoolan Devi's gang.

Behmai is a hamlet of nearly 300 households, precariously perched on the ravines of the Yamuna river – the southernmost part of the Chambal valley, notorious for its dacoit gangs since time immemorial. Besides subsistence agriculture, animal husbandry is the only source of livelihood for the Chaurasi Thakur community that dominates the village's social life. Those killed in the 1981 carnage included seventeen Thakurs, one Muslim, one Dalit, and one person belonging to the OBC (Other Backward Classes) community.

Contrary to generally held belief, the Chaurasi Thakurs of Behmai are not upper caste Thakurs, but reconverts from Islam who had been excommunicated by the Thakurs when they first embraced Islam. Unlike the regular Thakurs who have been the dominant landholders in the region for centuries, this community has fragmented landholdings and is confined to eighty-four ('chaurasi' in Hindi) villages in the Etawah, Kanpur Dehat, and Jalaun districts of the state. Although excommunicated from the Thakur community, this isolated group, whose members only marry amongst themselves, follows Brahmanical cultural norms characterised by an adherence to the practice of child marriage and opposition to widow remarriage.

The Behmai massacre went on to capture the imagination of the country. As the Phoolan Devi legend grew, movies came to be made and political parties became active here. But nobody cared to remember the condition of Behmai's widows. With no help coming from either the state or society, these women have now given up all hope of any redress.

In celluloid versions of the massacre – notably in filmmaker Shekhar Kapur's *Bandit Queen* – Behmai is invariably depicted as a village inhabited by brutal rapists, and this portrayal may have played a role in deflecting attention from the plight of its widows. Such portrayals seem to suggest that no one in such a decrepit village deserved any compensation. In politics, while prominent state leader Mulayam Singh Yadav's Samajwadi Party iconised Phoolan Devi as an OBC woman fighting for social justice, his rivals paraded the Behmai widows as part of their strategic counter-mobilisation of the upper caste Thakur communities. They even erected a shaheed sthal (martyrs' memorial) at the carnage site, where local politicians make ritualistic visits on February 14 every year.

But it is all shadow play. The continuing and unmitigated plight of these women represents the failure of the state and its criminal justice system. According to Bharat B. Das, author of *Victims in the Criminal Justice System*, "Victim's suffering, reparation and rehabilitation are essentially matters of the criminal justice system. Apart from undue hardships the victims face, failure on this count can result in their alienation and non-cooperation with the justice system or, worse, cause them to take law into their own hands."

This is exactly what happened in Behmai. To avenge the killing of Behmai's Thakurs, Phoolan Devi's rivals raided the neighbouring Astah village in Auraiya district, inhabited by people from her caste – the Mallahs – and perpetrated another massacre.

A growing number of experts feels that the Indian criminal justice system is oriented towards safeguarding the rights of offenders and not those of victims. Although there is provision for compensation to victims, the police, the judiciary as well as the state are primarily focused on the conviction of the offender. The classic study, *Compensation to the Victims of Dacoit Gangs in Chambal Valley*, by Saugar University sociologists D.P. Singh and D.R. Jatar, has highlighted this. After a scrutiny of 184 victims, the researchers found that the majority of them received either no compensation at all or merely paltry sums after considerable delay. "The victims, especially poor villagers, reported considerable difficulty in obtaining government help. They also complained that they had to bribe officials," wrote Singh and Jatar.

The Behmai widows present another dilemma. Since they are not perceived as the direct victims of the crimes perpetrated by the dacoits, they are not visible. Mahadei, the widow of Ram Singh Shakya, from an OBC background, underlined the poignancy of the situation she, and others like her, face: "When her man dies, a woman is invariably left to die forever."

Life in Salabila: No Relief from Relief Camps

Ratna Bharali Talukdar

Bongaigaon (Assam): The thatched shack with bamboo walls, measuring ten square feet, located in the Salabila relief camp in Assam's Bongaigaon district, was depressingly quiet. Poverty, hunger, and fatigue seemed to have blocked out the sounds that signify a happy home.

Marjina Khatun, 25, who lived there, looked exhausted. She had just returned home after a fourteen-hour shift at a construction site that casts slabs, and her youngest child, Manowar, aged eleven months, lay asleep on a mat on the floor, emaciated and naked.

While Marjina's life may appear as if it were a scene straight out of an 'alternative' film which had poverty as its backdrop, for her the privations were only too real. Just as they were for the scores of other Internally Displaced Persons (IDPs) – all Muslims – who had been languishing in the nine relief camps of Bongaigaon and Kokrajhar districts in Assam since 1993. When we visited the region in late 2009, these camps, housing 5,500 people, were located in Hapachara, Balajani, Tapatari, Salabila, and Bardhup in Bangaigaon district and in

Bangaldoba, Sanlatari, Nangalbhanga, and Bengtal in Kokrajhar.

Who were these people and why were they still living in the camps all these years later? It started way back in 1993 when the Bodo-led pro-statehood movement was at its peak. These people were uprooted from their ancestral villages, which numbered around forty-five across the two districts, following violent clashes between the Bodos – the single largest plains tribe in Assam – and the local migrant Muslim settlers. According to the records, sixty-four people of this community, chiefly poor farmers, were killed in Bangaigaon, while thirty-six died in Kokrajhar during that conflict. Many others were slain in sporadic incidents that followed between 1993 and 2000.

For Marjina, a mother of four, the conflict ended any chances she may have once had of living a fulfilled, happy life. She, and thousands of others like her, were reduced to becoming daily wage earners in the very region where they had once lived in self-sufficient ancestral homes and on the very land they had once farmed. In 2009, they were continuing to lead severely constricted lives in the absence of even the most basic amenities or social security.

Time and again, all attempts at rehabilitating this community were thwarted by hostile locals. For instance, in 2006, the Salabila inhabitants, who were earlier living in the Goroimari camp, were promised a permanent settlement because the Goroimari camp area had been acquired for expanding National Highway 31. The locals, however, opposed the move and the IDPs had to reconcile themselves to living in yet another makeshift camp, which came up at Salabila.

Salabila was typical of the nine relief camps functioning in the region. Spread over sixty-four bighas (one bigha equals 0.4 hectare), it was home to 1,310 families (over 6,500 people). Of the fifty-six tube wells provided by the government, only twenty-two were functional. As for toilets, while there were forty in all, many of them were clogged and unusable. Poor sanitary facilities and a critical water crisis had resulted in the practice of open defecation, which made for appallingly unhygienic conditions. According to camp dwellers, the hot summer months and the rainy season were the worst times of the year, with children, in particular, falling gravely ill because of the environment in which they were living.

Sarbeswar Bayan, a surveillance worker at the nearby Dompara Mini Public Health Centre (PHC), spoke of the severe health crisis that people were up against. According to him, while living in unhygienic conditions increased the chances of diseases like chicken pox, malaria, diarrhoea, jaundice, and other water-borne infections taking on epidemic proportions, for the inmates at Salabila the situation was even worse because there was no health care facility to cater to their needs apart from a doctor who visited the local PHC once a week. Moreover, travelling to nearby towns for medical treatment was not really an option, given the distances entailed and the fact that every working day lost meant a significant loss of income.

Without a doubt, children were the worst affected. As food was hard to come by – the rice provided to each family lasted for only ten days a month – around 1,639 children in the 0-14 years age group showed signs of malnutrition.

Failing health apart, even their education was at risk. In fact, for an entire decade – between 1993 and 2003 – many of the children had not even stepped into a classroom. It was only after the Sarva Shiksha Abhiyan – the government's flagship programme for the time-bound achievement of universal primary education – decided to set up a centre in Goroimari under the Education Guarantee Scheme, that some form of schooling was made available to them. At Salabila, two Sanyogi Siksha Kendras (SSKs) – which are usually meant for out-of-school children, but serve as formal schools in such camps – were providing primary education. A total of 543 primary students were enrolled in 2010, being taught by six teachers who were paid an extremely nominal salary of Rs 1,500 per month.

As for the government-run Mid-Day Meal Scheme (MDM), only one of the two functioning SSKs had been covered, revealed Amir Hussain, a teacher and secretary of the local camp management committee. He also added that the rations provided under the MDM scheme were often inadequate: at the SSK where he taught, of the 419 students enrolled, only 279 could be provided with a meal.

Also missing from the camp was an anganwadi centre (government-run crèche), mandated to care for children in the 0-6 years age group, lactating mothers, pregnant women, and underweight adolescent girls, under the Supplementary Nutritional Programme of the Integrated Children Development Scheme.

There was a clear lack of focus in addressing the urgent problems faced by women and children, perhaps because there were no women holding important positions within camp management committees. It wasn't as if they were incapable of taking decisions or getting things done, it was just that they were not being given a chance.

Yet, women had stepped up to contribute in more ways than one. Besides taking care of her home and family, Marjina was one of the several women here who had also become a breadwinner for her family. A typical work day for this hard-working woman started early in the morning when she boarded the overcrowded truck arranged by contractors to transport workers to distant construction sites for slab-casting work.

While this kind of work was better paid than others, it also involved great uncertainty as the enormous demand for wage work ensured that jobs were not easy to come by. Marjina said that she got Rs 100 per day and some extra money for overtime duty. "Normally, I get work like this for ten to twelve days each month," she added. Another fallout of the employment crisis was that children were often forced to discontinue school after they completed the primary levels, as they were expected to help out at home, with both parents away the whole day looking for work.

Nearly two decades had passed since Marjina first moved to Salabila and she had no idea how many more years she would have to spend in this ghetto. Normalcy was what everybody at the camp longed for. Hope kept alternating with despair. The words of young Hamida, who had grown up as an IDP at Salabila, said it all: "Over nearly two decades, many people visited us, sometimes at the Bongaigaon relief camp, sometimes in Goroimari, and sometimes here. They all talked of giving us a settled space, but wherever we moved, there was always local protest against our presence. I have seen how young girls are practically sold in the camps in the name of marriage. Getting two meals, some education, a few clothes are all luxuries for us. Are the lives we lead here normal?"

When Women Take Up Arms

Soma Mitra

Paschim Medinipur (West Bengal): In the summer of 2009, conflict in Lalgarh, in West Bengal's West Midnapore district (now called Paschim Medinipur), had reached a point of no return. By late June, Operation Lalgarh, an armed intervention by central government forces against Maoist insurgents in the region, in tandem with the state police, was in full swing. A nondescript area became a battleground, and its poverty-stricken inhabitants were either drawn into the violent confrontation between security forces and Maoist insurgents or caught in the crossfire.

What was striking about the Lalgarh developments was the mass mobilisation of women, many of whom joined the ranks of the Maoists after their sons and husbands were arrested by the police for being sympathetic to the insurgency. The women even participated as members of 'peasant battalions' – wielding bows and arrows, even axes, and raising slogans, staging rallies, and participating in acts of arson.

How did this come about? Why did ordinary women find it necessary to take up arms? At one level, the events that played out in Lalgarh could be seen as a battle between the ruling West Bengal government and its party, the Communist Party of India (Marxist) [CPI(M)], and the insurgent Maoists, assisted by the People's Committee Against Police Atrocities (PCAPA). At another level, it was about the discontent of a troubled community fighting for survival and the basic necessities of life, such as potable water and education for its children, which found expression in public protests.

Talking to these women in the turbulent days of June 2009 revealed just how stark was the local deprivation. Shashi Murmu, 28, of Mulapara village in the adjoining Shalboni block of East Midnapore district (now called Purba Medinipur), spoke for many women in the region when she said, "We don't have clean drinking water; our children are deprived of proper schools. We have no other way but to revolt against this situation." Her mother, Tara, 51, who also took up arms, added, "For a long while, we have been forced to lead a miserable existence. That's why we have decided that from now we will fight." Almost everybody in Mulapara had a similar view.

What was most striking was the fact that these women were completely fearless. They did not appear to be scared of any police reaction to their protests. Even earlier, the villagers in these areas revealed, the police had often picked them up for questioning whenever there was a Maoist attack. As soon as the combined operations were announced, the men had fled the villages, leaving the women behind to face the wrath of the security forces. While the police claim that they did not generally pick up women for interrogation, the people here told another story, adding that there was little administrative recourse or legal support when harsh and unjust treatment was meted out.

Government agencies were shaken when images of local women with arms began flooding the media, and a six-member delegation was sent to assess the actual situation on the ground. The experiences of this delegation proved to be a major eye-opener. R.D. Meena, Secretary, Backward Classes

Welfare, who was a member of the delegation, is reported to have said, "I was shocked to see many [people] are yet to get ration cards. Those who should have rightly been enlisted as Below Poverty Line [BPL] are listed as Above Poverty Line."

Employment – or rather the lack of it – was a huge source of local discontent. Said Gouri Mahato, when we met her in 2009 at her village, Domahani, which lies close to Lalgarh, "The panchayat [village council] had assured my family of a job card under the rural jobs guarantee programme [the Mahatma Gandhi National Rural Employment Guarantee Act, 2005 (MGNREGA)] two years ago. But I have not got one till date." MGNREGA assures the rural household of a minimum of 100 days of unskilled wage work in a year.

Gouri's family had five bighas of land (one bigha equals 0.4 hectare), which they were forced to sell off when her mother fell critically ill and had to be taken to a Kolkata hospital for treatment because the primary health centre at Lalgarh had no doctor on duty. At the time, a job card could have made all the difference to Gouri.

Other women, like Krishna Halder, considered themselves 'luckier'. Halder did get a job card issued to her, but she had managed to access only fourteen days of work over the last two years. Eventually, the struggle of daily life took its toll on Krishna's family. Her son joined the PCAPA and, later, the ranks of the Maoists, before being taken into police custody.

Earlier, the villages of Paschim Medinipur district were the stronghold of the CPI(M). However, three decades of rule by its government had left Lalgarh without a proper irrigation system and other necessary infrastructure. A large section of people were still dependent on forest produce for their livelihood, including women like Mohua Baskey, who went into the forest every day at about five in the morning to collect kendu pata (leaves used to roll tobacco to make the local cigarettes called beedis). Baskey's teenaged daughter accompanied her on this daily two-kilometre walk into the woods to supplement the family's meagre income. According to Baskey, the early morning toil of these two women and their subsequent trip to the market resulted in a paltry Rs 15 each day, which was obviously insufficient for their family of four. When Baskey was asked why she hadn't bothered to get her daughter educated, her explanation was matter-of-fact. "If I allow my daughter to go to school, our income, which is already such a pittance, would be reduced by half," she said.

The other major concern voiced by women here was corruption in the Public Distribution System (PDS). Said one old woman, "We have nothing else but our ration cards to give us something to put into our stomachs." Unfortunately, as Meena noted during his fact-finding mission, the PDS system was in a shambles, as illustrated by the case of around 400 families of Gopalpur village. As all the households in the village fell into the BPL category, they were supposed to get twenty-five kilograms of rice at a rate of Rs 2.50 a month. However, the women complained that the local ration dealers claimed that they were entitled to only ten kilograms of rice a month. Moreover, as standard practice, these ration dealers – many of whom were either members of the ruling party or were well-connected with government officials – insisted on retaining everybody's ration cards so that they could dole out a small proportion of their entitlements to them every month. It was not surprising to see evidence of malnutrition on the faces and bodies of most children in these villages.

When the women of Lalgarh took up arms and joined the ranks of the insurgents, it made for striking media coverage. But it was also a searing comment on their lives, for behind each of those images of women holding aloft machetes was a terrible – and preventable – human tragedy.

How Lalgarh's Flames Engulfed Ordinary Lives

Ajitha Menon

Paschim Medinipur (West Bengal): What began as a landmine attack on the convoy of West Bengal Chief Minister Buddhadeb Bhattacharya in late 2008, rapidly escalated into a spiral of violence that affected large swathes of the district of Paschim Medinipur, perpetrated by the state police, on the one hand, and Maoist cadres, claiming to represent the interests of the local tribal population, on the other. The Lok Sabha elections of 2009 only fanned the stand-off that had as its epicentre the village of Lalgarh, in Binpur-I block, located in the Jhargram subdivision of the district.

By June 2009, special central forces were assisting the state police in Operation Lalgarh, a consolidated armed intervention against the Maoists operating in the area. The Maoists, in turn, were assisted by a group that called itself the People's Committee Against Police Atrocities (PCAPA). The conflict carried on for months thereafter, deeply impacting the lives of ordinary people. For the women, in particular, it was a period of great distress.

When we reached Lalgarh in June 2009, about 35,000 people had already fled what came to be known as the Pirakata-Ramgarh-Goaltore triangular war zone. Many had taken shelter in state relief camps; others found temporary accommodation in the homes of relatives. With violence a constant threat, schools everywhere were closed and, what was worse, nobody could go out to work to keep their families fed.

Mangala Mal and Savitri Murmu were two women who found themselves on opposing sides of this conflict. They were divided by age as well as by ideology, but the consequences of the conflict for both were eerily similar. Both had been abused and tortured, both had lost their homes.

For Mangala, 26, the nightmare started in December 2008,

when PCAPA-supported Maoists entered her village of Pirrakuli and started recruiting reluctant villagers for their cause. "They announced that there would be a police boycott and they wanted the men to join their force, apparently to protect villages. But the men were taken into jungles and forced to fight the police and the administration. My husband, a Communist Party of India (Marxist) [CPI(M)] cadre, was taken away. I never saw him again. I was beaten and molested when my husband refused to go with them, so he had no choice but to leave," she recalled with tears in her eyes.

On the other hand, Savitri, 60, willingly joined the PCAPA after she was tortured by the police following the fateful landmine blast. "I wanted to take revenge for the abuse and took part in all the PCAPA rallies. I was there when the police camp at Shirish was set on fire," she told us. This meant that when the central government forces took control of the area again, Savitri found herself on the police hit list.

Savitri elaborated: "The Central Reserve Police Force [CRPF] came looking for my son, Dulal, on June 18, 2009, when they launched the operation. They called him a Maoist and threatened to kill me if I did not inform them about his movements. I had to hide in the jungles at night and during the day come back to my village where people offered me protection." The uncertainty of her son's fate made her sick. All she wanted was for the violence to end.

In any conflict, the consequences for women are the same, whichever side they are on. When Operation Lalgarh commenced, Kamala Mal, 48, fled with her family of six from Pirrakuli village on foot, since there was no public transport plying once the security operations were in full swing. "We had been living in terror. The Maoists came and forced the men to go with them. When my husband, Gopal, refused, he was beaten. Then the armed men turned on me and my daughter-in-law, who was breast-feeding her three-month-old baby. They left only after we gave them Rs 50 and two kilograms of rice. But we knew they would return. That's why we decided to leave," she said.

When Kamala Mal's family fled their home, they left behind eight bighas of land (one bigha equals 0.4 hectare), paddy stock, and Gopal's eighty-four-year-old mother. "She could hardly walk. How could she cover the distance to Medinipur on foot?" asked Gopal. He was clearly heartbroken over her fate, but almost every family in the village had left the old, the infirm, and the cattle behind, not knowing what would happen to them.

Mangala also quit her village when the central forces took control of the highway in June. For her, paying the Maoists their daily collection of Rs 20 and one kilogram of rice was a huge burden. But the last straw was when they wanted her to join them in their fight. "They used women and children as a frontline resistance force. Refusal led to severe beatings. But I had to think of my six-year-old daughter," she said.

Where some families were fed up with the diktat of the Maoists, others shed light on police brutality. Said Sandhya Manna, 34, of Shirish village, "Traditionally, women here earned money by collecting sal leaves from the Anandapur forest, which are then made into leaf plates. But, for months we were unable to go into the forests because of a police camp there. The policemen would harass us – I know of cases where women have faced brutal assaults at their hands."

Incidents like these only served to inflame popular anger against the police in the region and led to the burning down of CPI(M) party offices and police camps. Bedona Mahato, 68, the mother of PCAPA leader Chatradhar Mahato, talked in detail about police brutality. She said, "The police used to pick up young men from our villages and accuse them of being Maoists. They never returned. Their mothers and wives can only feel hatred towards them. My son is in hiding, but I keep up the resistance despite the repeated raids and torture."

The active participation of women was a conspicuous aspect of the Lalgarh interregnum. Explained Monglee, of Chotopelia village, "Many young women like me voluntarily joined the PCAPA. We are peace-loving, but we won't be treated like second-class citizens. Our demands are simple: we want safe drinking water, water for irrigation, and an end to corruption in the administration. But nobody listens."

Some women were openly militant. "We have our traditional weapons like bows and arrows, the spade, and sickle. If necessary, we can fight for ages to safeguard our rights," said Esha Mari, 58, of Shirish village. But even as she said this, she added, "We know that prosperity for our children will only come with peace. We just want both sides to recognise our right to live decent lives."

Ultimately, no one in this region had escaped the terrible impact of that spell of violence. Lalgarh was full of sad stories of women. Of Jharna Mal, 25, who was waiting interminably for her husband, Manoranjan, to return – he had been picked up by the police one night for questioning from her village of Pathardanga, two kilometres from Lalgarh; of Pingbani village's Lakshmi Soren, who cried out that her family had nowhere to go because her husband and sons were being threatened by the Maoists for not having joined them. Like Mangala Mal and Savitri Murmu, although they found themselves on opposing sides, the trauma that this conflict had wrought was remarkably similar.

Barred from Life: Experiences of Women Prisoners

Anjali Singh

Lucknow (Uttar Pradesh): With tears streaming down her wrinkled face, Geeta Devi (name changed), 70, asked plaintively, "Bhagwan ne is umar mein mujhe itna dukh kyun diya hai?" (Why has God given me so much sorrow at my advanced age?)

Geeta's grievance against fate was not completely baseless. Convicted by the court of Shahjahanpur, a small district in Uttar Pradesh, she was serving a life sentence under Section

498A of the Indian Penal Code. In jail for the past eight years, the old woman, who was incapable even of standing straight when we met her in 2011, had only painful memories to keep her company. All her thoughts were focused on her two young grandsons, whom she had brought to the Nari Bandi Grah (women's penitentiary) at the Adarsh Jail (Model Prison), on the outskirts of state capital, Lucknow, when she was sentenced. They too had been taken away from her and placed in a protection home for children above six years of age.

Geeta recalled the fateful day that brought her world crashing down: "My mother had passed away and I had gone to the next village for her cremation. When I came back, I was arrested by the police and sent to jail. I was told that my daughter-in-law's family had filed an FIR [First Information Report] against the whole family, under Section 498A. I did not even get time to consult a lawyer. My son was also arrested and sent to the Bareilly jail. I was forced to bring both my grandsons – just two- and four-years-old then – to jail. They grew up here, but have been sent away to a protection home now. My family is completely destroyed. I just hope God will do justice one day before I die."

Condemned and lonely, Geeta's condition was quite miserable. But she was not alone. Behind the walls of the newly-constructed Adarsh Jail at Mohanlal Ganj, were many women and children whose fate had been sealed with pain, stress, and ill-health. Many among them also claimed they were suffering the ignominy for no fault of their own – that they were truly innocent. Narrated a vehement Krishna Kanta, 25, from Sonebhadra district, who was serving a life sentence for allegedly murdering her husband: "I was just seventeen and one month pregnant when Naxalites came to our hut one night. They locked me in the next room and hacked my husband to death. I kept screaming for help, but no one from the village came forward. Next morning, the police arrived and arrested me because the villagers gave witness that I had murdered my husband. My son was born in jail and was taken away to a protection home when he was six. Every day I think of him. He was not even born when all this happened, he doesn't deserve the life of a convict."

Shunned and rebuked by society, Adarsh Jail's women convicts had no choice but to suffer silently. What tormented them most was being separated from their families, particularly their children. And while they may have reconciled themselves to their situation, they were fiercely against their children being forced to spend their lives in jails and protection homes. Of course, the constant agonising had taken a toll on their health, with most showing signs of mental and physical breakdown.

Explained Indu Mati Singh, deputy jailor of Nari Bandi Grah in 2011, "The aim of this new jail was to make life a little easier for women serving prolonged jail terms. But I have seen that though we may give them the best of everything, it can never compensate for the loss of freedom and separation from children. Most inmates suffer from depression and anxiety, and are receiving regular treatment at the jail hospital. Carrying the stigma of being a convict ruins any chance of their going back home and into the society they once knew. This realisation has an added emotional burden. It's a very sad state to be living in."

While the younger women were trying to take control of their lives and health, the older inmates suffered greatly because age was not on their side. "When they are sent in at the age of sixty or seventy," said Singh, "the confinement breaks their resolve and spirit. They age faster and can't even walk to the toilet on their own. Many old women prisoners who can't see in the night have fallen and hurt themselves. We try to ensure that someone accompanies them at night, but it's not possible to keep a constant vigil."

An ailing Geeta was surviving on the medical attention she received from the jail hospital staff. She needed the support of the prison walls to walk even a few steps. Then there was Sharda Devi, 80, from Kanpur, who, on her way to the privy one night, had fallen and broken her knee. Sentenced to life under Section 498A, she had already served ten years when this happened. Since her accident, Sharda had been languishing in the jail hospital, her body covered with bedsores. She broke down as she said, "I wish I were dead." The nurses, too, were not able to do much to ease her condition. Said Kirti (name changed), a nurse who had seen Sharda deteriorate, "The emotional torture is the most difficult for her to bear. Besides, it is very difficult for bones to heal at this age. What is really sad is that she has ten years more to go in jail, so she can't even be sent home to be cared for by her family. It's difficult seeing old prisoners suffer like this."

As grim as all this may sound, most inmates were grateful that they had access to a well-run hospital within the jail. What disturbed them greatly, though, was the extreme lack of sensitivity on the part of the legal system. Dulari (name changed), 26, an inmate from Lalitpur district, said, "I had just given birth to my son at my mother's house when I got the news that my husband had been attacked and killed by his elder brother. The reason was a long-standing land dispute, so I was shocked when the police came and arrested me for the crime. Even the judge refused to listen to me and I was sentenced to life under Section 302 [of the Indian Penal Code]. I have already served ten years and till date have had no access to a lawyer. I miss my child the most and I blame the legal system for ruining many young lives like my own."

G. Sreedevi, a senior bureaucrat who once headed the Uttar Pradesh State Legal Services Authority, agreed with Dulari. "When I hear such stories and meet women in jail, I am shocked. I think judicial officers need to be more sensitive in cases where there is a possibility, however remote, of the accused being innocent. Committing a woman to life imprisonment is like giving her a death sentence, especially when she has young children," she commented.

R.K. Mittal, former special secretary and DG Prisons, district jail, Lucknow, who has written a book on his experiences with prisoners, put it thus: "Life in jail changes people, it breaks their spirit, and cuts them off from everything that has meant something to them. Women suffer more since they feel they have so much to lose apart from their freedom."

From the Streets to Jail: Painful Transitions

Shwetha E. George

Kottayam (Kerala): What did Meenakshi, Sarojini, and Rakkamma have in common? All three were Tamil-speaking women, under forty years of age, and living under one roof. They were inmates of the women's cell at the Kottayam sub-jail. Accused of petty theft, all three were migrants – among the many who come to Kerala from neighbouring states. During the summers, these women cross the border to make some quick money on the streets of Kerala's cities, but many end up behind bars. Of the eleven inmates in the Kottayam jail in mid-2011 – all of them undertrials – nine were arrested this way.

Although they were extremely reluctant to speak about their lives, when coaxed to do so, they came out with accounts that were remarkably similar.

Rakkamma, 35, a native of Pollachi in Coimbatore district of Tamil Nadu, had been coming to central Kerala for a few months every year to beg in the small town of Changanasserry. Usually, she brought her toddler along with her during these excursions, while leaving behind her four school-going children to be looked after by her mother and husband, an umbrella hawker.

In the summer of 2011, Rakkamma's mother and twelve-year-old daughter decided to spend time with her, sharing her dingy shack located at one end of the public grounds in Kottayam. On the day she was arrested, Rakkamma and her daughter were begging at different points near the busy bus station area, when, as she put it, there was "suddenly a hue and cry and, before I knew it, the crowd was dragging my daughter to the police station". Eventually, Rakkamma said, she was arrested instead of her daughter.

Immediately afterwards, her mother left town with Rakkamma's daughter and baby. Rakkamma was left to fend for herself alone in jail. She didn't even know who her court-appointed lawyer was, let alone his contact number. "No one has come for me in the last two months. I don't know how long I'll be here," she said.

Meenakshi, too, was extremely downcast because no one from her family had bothered to visit her at the sub-jail. She constantly remembered her three children who were living with her mother in Chennai. "They haven't come even once. I have no one to help me. Maybe it's better they don't see me like this," she said. Meenakshi and her nineteen-year-old married sister, Sarojini, were nabbed from the bus stop at Pampady, a village near Kottayam. She insisted they were innocent. "I saw a chain on the ground and picked it up when everyone just pounced on me and my sister and took us to the station," she maintained.

According to Ratnakumari, the jail matron of the Kottayam sub-jail in 2011, some of the women undertrials were actually victims of a huge begging racket being controlled by a gang leader and his agents. These agents always ensured that the women were eventually released. "One agent visits an inmate, claiming to be her brother, and, two months later, he is back to visit another one of his so-called sisters. It's a mutually beneficial relationship: the women earn a steady daily wage, while those who run the operation get the women's earnings," she revealed.

The women, however, denied any such connections, although Meenakshi did reveal that she was able to earn around Rs 300 a day if she begged on the streets with her toddler. She added that a toddler accompanied by a ten-year-old girl could collect up to Rs 200 per day.

Jayashankar, an advocate at the Kerala State Legal Services Authority at Kottayam, felt strongly that the police must deport these petty criminals back to their places of origin, rather than keep them incarcerated. His reasons were straightforward: first, court procedures are tedious and costly. Second, there is a serious space crunch in the women's jail. With only three cells available, accommodating these women is a major problem. Third, and most important, the police need to recognise that these women are driven by poverty to do what they do and that they were certainly not professional criminals. "Most arrive here by default. Either they have lost all their money and cannot buy a return ticket, so they stick around and get caught while stealing. Or they come as a couple to work in Kerala and, after an ugly domestic spat, the wife finds herself abandoned with the children and with no means to return home. She is practically forced by circumstances to resort to stealing," Jayashankar observed.

Having studied the situation, Jayashankar also believed that most women migrants who were first-time offenders rarely came back to Kerala once they were acquitted. "Unfortunately, however, acquittals are very rare in the crime of theft because the evidence recovery has already happened. This means that these women have to serve a seven-year sentence," he said.

Sections 379 and 380 of the Indian Penal Code state that attempted theft and theft can earn a sentence of three and seven years respectively, if there is a conviction. These are both non-bailable offences, which means that bail can be set only at the discretion of the court, depending on the nature of the offence. The undertrials are taken to court every fifteen days, which is the remand period under the Criminal Procedure Code, and returned to jail until the trial date is set, the trial carried out, and the verdict declared.

"What we need is classification of crime and criminals in our jail system," said Jayashankar. He argued that habitual offenders, first-time offenders, and teenage offenders should be incarcerated in separate jails, and that a first-time offender should not be allowed to be in close proximity with habitual offenders because she may end up getting drawn into criminal networks and committing even worse crimes. "Also, a criminal's detention space should depend on the nature of a crime. It is not right to have a woman accused of infanticide, for instance, share the same cell as another accused of major theft," he added.

If life outside the prison walls was tough, owing to poverty and destitution, then life behind them was very traumatic. These women were paying a heavy price for their incarceration – physically, mentally, and emotionally – not knowing when they would finally be set free. Most women prisoners spent much of their time moping about their children and worrying about their welfare. In fact, most had got into this sorry situation precisely because they imagined they could improve their families' circumstances by resorting to theft. Of course, what hurt most was that their family members seemed to have deserted them, leaving them helpless and isolated. Said a tearful Ammalu, 25, who admitted that she was caught pickpocketing, "We do it only to save our children from starvation." While she was serving time in prison, her three-year-old was in an orphanage in Kottayam and, according to Ammalu's friend and cellmate, they had been told that her daughter cried for her mother every day.

So what is the day like for a prison inmate? Meenakshi, the most open of them all, put it very starkly: "We simply talk. We eat our three meals. We cry ourselves to sleep." They hadn't given the jail authorities any cause for complaint, and Ratnakumari vouched for their discipline. "I haven't had any problem with them," she said. "They keep themselves and their room clean."

In mid-2011, Meenakshi, Sarojini, and Rakkamma were preparing to be produced in court, but nobody was expecting a miracle. "The judge will look up, write something down, and then put us away," said a dejected Meenakshi, adding that this had been their routine every fifteen days.

Despair was evident in the very language of these three women. Truly, the walls that surrounded them had come to define the limits of their life.

Conviction and Courage Keep Wives of Political Prisoners Going

Sharmistha Choudhury

Kolkata (West Bengal): In West Bengal, especially in the state capital of Kolkata, fervent celebrations mark the five days of Durga Puja, an important annual Hindu festival. But the last time Shikha Sen Roy enjoyed Durga Puja festivities was in 2001, when her husband, Himadri Sen Roy (alias Somen), the jailed Maoist leader and ex-state secretary of the West Bengal committee of the Communist Party of India (Maoist), was still with the family.

Post-2001, Himadri went underground and then, on February 23, 2007, he was arrested and put in prison. Since then, life has turned into a grim battle for Shikha. "Although he had been away from home for years, I was happy because he was free. He was fighting against an unjust system. But now he's in poor health and it tortures me to think that he has been robbed of the one thing a person treasures the most: liberty," said Shikha, sitting in her modest one-room home in the city in late 2011.

Besides the emotional trauma, Shikha was also struggling with numerous health problems. She was chronically underweight, under constant medication, and even came very close to a nervous breakdown once. "I couldn't have afforded medical treatment if it hadn't been for our family physician who respects my husband and refuses to accept any fees from me," she said, adding, "Yet, I often skip the medicines he prescribes because I simply cannot pay for them. But that's no big deal. The vast majority of people in our country cannot afford any health care at all." What was far more important to Shikha was ensuring that she could buy her husband the little things he needed in jail: clothes, dry rations, and books.

An activist with a local women's organisation, Shikha didn't like talking about her own situation. Yet, one look at the dreary single room that was her home, dominated by a rickety sewing machine that provided her her daily bread – she is a ladies' tailor by profession – a small bed, a gas oven, and a couple of plastic chairs, left little doubt of the wretchedness of her situation. But she chose to remain positive, believing that there were others who were far worse off than her. Perhaps women like Mukta Chakraborty, the wife of jailed Maoist leader and spokesman, Gour Chakraborty.

A pall of gloom hung over Mukta's tiny home in the suburb of Madanpur, a few kilometres from Kolkata, as her only son, Somprakash, too, had been arrested on suspicion of being involved in Maoist activities and sent to the neighbouring state of Jharkhand. Last heard, he was lodged in prison in Jamshedpur. Her voice shaking with anger and despair, the elderly lady said, "First it was my husband and now my son. What was his crime? Joining the campaign for the release of all political prisoners, including his father? That alone made him a dangerous terrorist? Why don't they pick me up too and round off the score?"

Mukta, who was working in a small medicine factory for paltry wages, was entitled to only one day off in a week. "But I have already used up all my leave visiting my husband in jail, consulting lawyers, being present in court for case hearings, and participating in campaigns demanding his release. So now my wages are deducted when I take time off. At this rate, how will I meet my husband and son who are in jail in two different states? I'm really at the end of my tether," she rued. She said that while she could bear most things, what she couldn't was to see her once lively and spirited husband confined to prison, ailing and weak, with the hope of freedom steadily fading away.

Mahamaya Sarkar, the wife of jailed Maoist leader Chandi Sarkar, was also struggling to put up a brave front. After the West Bengal assembly elections were held, there had been a ray of hope when the state government announced that fifty-odd prisoners, including Sarkar, were slated to be released soon. "My daughter and I were so happy. I thought that that was to be the Trinamool Congress government's first step in honouring its electoral promise of releasing all political prisoners. I couldn't wait for my husband to come home...it's been seven years and he is really old and ill now," she said. Her happiness was short-lived as the government announced it would not be releasing any Maoist leaders because of strong reservations conveyed to it by the central government on the issue.

Thereafter, things went from bad to worse for Mahamaya. Earlier, her husband was lodged in Krishnanagar prison in Nadia district – where she lived in a tumbledown house with her only daughter – and she could visit him often and keep an eye on his health. Then he was transferred to Dumdum jail in Kolkata. The authorities suspected him of inspiring fellow prisoners to protest against the abysmal quality of the food and the high-handedness of prison officials. "I can't visit him regularly now," said Mahamaya. "It takes nearly three hours to reach Kolkata by train. If I take time off from my small sari business, how will I earn?"

Once every fortnight, Mahamaya travelled to Kolkata to buy saris in bulk from traders and then hauled them back to sell in Krishnanagar. Of course, when a lot went unsold, she would lug it back to exchange for newer goods. It was hard work and it only got harder when she had to fit regular visits to Dumdum jail into her schedule. "My husband continues to be ill, but I have been able to visit him only once since," she sighed.

These brave women were aware that it would be easy for their husbands to get bail if they publicly renounced their ideals and promised to cooperate with the government. But not one of them wanted her husband to take such a step. They were unanimous in the opinion that 'surrender' is a hateful word. "The police have raided my home twice: once before my husband's arrest and once after," recounted Shikha. "They ransacked the single room in which I live with my son, interrogated me mercilessly, and took away dozens of books and every single photo that I had of my husband. The second time, they came in the dead of night and accused me of sheltering Maoist activists! I know I can be arrested at any time. I certainly wouldn't have borne all these trials if I had wanted my husband to surrender," she declared.

In Mahamaya's case, after her husband's arrest, she had to spend many days away from home because the police would turn up at odd hours for questioning. Even her minor daughter was not spared. Some weeks later, she too was arrested on suspicion of having links with Maoists, but was released when the charges could not be proved. "I shall never forget those days in police custody and the torture that I had to face," she said.

In 2011, in a fresh bid to secure the freedom of political prisoners, Shikha had taken the initiative to bring together various women's organisations and the wives of political prisoners onto a single platform to demand the unconditional release of not just Maoists, but all political prisoners. She stated, "We will start a vigorous campaign soon. Political prisoners are not criminals and we are proud to be fighting for them."

Arrested Lives: When Trade Union Struggles Came Home

Sharmistha Choudhury

North 24 Parganas (West Bengal): Saraswati is only twenty-seven. Yet, except when she smiles, she looks older. She has been through an unending cycle of hope and despair – mostly despair – over the past five years: her husband, a jute mill trade unionist, was first sent to jail for murder, then dismissed from service after being released on bail, reinstated after a year of fierce struggle, and then booked again on charges of attempted murder, and dismissed from service yet again. He has since been released from jail, but this experience has aged Saraswati more than an entire lifetime.

Her story is important because it is the story of innumerable women across India whose husbands, fathers or brothers find themselves in prison for their trade union activities. What are the experiences of such women? How do they cope? How do they fight suicidal thoughts and keep going?

Returning to Saraswati's story, it was in 2008 that her husband, Rajkumar Singh, 29, a worker in a prominent jute mill in the North 24 Parganas district of West Bengal, first dared to take up the cudgels against the mill authorities. He was joined by a few fearless colleagues. Together, they demanded that retired workers be paid gratuity dues and that the Provident Fund accounts of all workers be made public. The mill authorities didn't want to do that, perhaps because a large chunk of their profits came from depriving workers of their legitimate entitlements. Instead, the management came down heavily on Singh and his friends for taking up this issue.

"I knew what my husband was doing involved a lot of risk. His company was notorious for ruthlessly suppressing workers' movements. So I expected him to be beaten up or sacked any day," recalled this mother of four, sitting in her modest home in 2011, her children huddled around her.

What Saraswati hadn't expected was that her husband would be falsely implicated in a murder case. In May 2008, Singh – along with nineteen others – was booked under Section 302 of the Indian Penal Code and jailed on charges of murder. It took them three months to manage to raise bail and get out of prison. "Those were the worst days of my life," said Saraswati, adding, "There was no money. The kids often went without food when shopkeepers refused to extend credit. The electricity was disconnected because of non-payment."

According to Salma Khatun, the wife of Peer Mohammed, who was a colleague and cellmate of Singh's, "The trauma was worse than the hunger. As the court dismissed one bail plea after another, I was certain my husband would remain imprisoned for years. I couldn't eat or sleep, imagining the worst." Her daughter was just a year old and those bleak days had a profound impact on the infant. With her father no longer around and her mother always crying instead of playing with her, the child slowly fell silent, her once-cherubic face robbed of its normal cheer. Only months after her father was released from jail did her peals of laughter ring out in their tiny home once again.

"I knew my brother and his friends were no criminals – they had to go to jail because they had the temerity to demand their basic rights," asserted Basanti, sister of Shyam Sundar Shaw, the leader of the agitating workers, with pride in her voice. "Just the previous year, the mill authorities had pressurised the local police to arrest him for his alleged involvement in a dacoity case. He spent a fortnight in jail before the case was dismissed. All the workers of this mill, especially the old and ailing ones, love him. If it hadn't been for their support, my brother may still have been in jail," she added. Basanti was engaged to be married at the time of Shaw's arrest, but the engagement was called off when it was learnt that the bride-to-be's brother was in prison.

For the families of Shaw and his comrades-in-arms, there was little relief when they were finally released on bail. The mill authorities refused to give them back their jobs. A year of fierce struggle followed and, once again, Saraswati was on tenterhooks. She was petrified that her husband would be sent to jail again on another fabricated charge.

Moreover, with Singh jobless, their daily struggles were already unbearable: the children had to be taken out of school and two meals a day were a luxury for the family. The local doctor, too, bluntly refused to treat them on credit. When the hungry children fell ill with alarming regularity, Saraswati recalled that she often had a mad urge to run away. "I even entertained thoughts of taking my two youngest and jumping in front of a speeding train to end it all," she confessed.

But despite the utter ruination they faced, the indomitable young trade unionists didn't give up. They picketed the mill, held countless meetings and demonstrations, went on hunger strikes, and made public the manner in which the authorities were siphoning off funds from workers' accounts. The struggle finally bore fruit. The sitting Member of Parliament (MP) of the constituency was defeated in the Lok Sabha election of 2009 and the new MP promised to taken action. Singh and his friends were reinstated by a very reluctant management.

Back at work, they did not abandon their mission. Said Salma with a lingering smile, "I knew the workers of the mill regarded my husband as their hero, but that hardly helped when there was no food in the house or when my mother-in-law needed hospitalisation because her blood pressure shot up due to anxiety over her son's fate."

In 2010, the mill authorities, desperate for a solution, conceded a few of the workers' demands. They began to issue gratuity payments to a slew of retired workers. There was a whiff of victory in the air. "But I knew things would not remain rosy," sighed Salma. Sure enough, after a few months, the authorities stopped issuing gratuity payments. The battle began all over again.

In mid-January 2011, First Information Reports were lodged against the trade unionists at the local police station. They were booked on charges of "attempt to murder". Apparently, they had 'attempted to murder' a senior manager of the mill, although he had not suffered a scratch. "Our husbands had no choice but to abscond," said Saraswati, "they became fugitives from the law."

It was a long time before the men were able to secure anticipatory bail. But for their wives, mothers, and sisters, the trauma was no less this time round. Salma was at a critical stage of her pregnancy. Saraswati's eldest son, around ten-years-old, took to petty crime. Basanti was resigned to a life of drudgery, with her mother taking to her bed and the burden of supporting the family falling on her frail shoulders.

Although the men eventually managed bail, their fight is far from over and, although their lawyers have been extremely kind and accommodating, financial pressures are acute. Singh's children still do not go to school; Peer's newborn daughter is an underweight baby, in and out of hospital. Uncertainty continues to dog the life of women like Saraswati and Salma, who live with the fear that their husbands could be thrown into prison at any point and perhaps never come out.

But if there is anything that these women have learnt from the experiences of the past years, it is the importance of coming together and speaking out. Saraswati, for one, has promised herself that should her husband and his colleagues get jailed again, she will personally take to the streets with her four children in tow, to demand justice.

Behind Police Lines: Edgy Lives of Constables' Wives

Shwetha George

Kottayam (Kerala): While the media's focus has invariably been on police atrocities, not enough attention has been paid to the poor conditions under which police personnel at the lower levels of the constabulary live and work – factors that could play a part in triggering police brutality. A constable's job is a highly coveted one in a state like Kerala, with its high unemployment figures. Yet, life in the barracks is often far from congenial.

The struggle begins the moment the Public Service Commission examination results are announced. A successful recruit is faced with an extremely gruelling training programme at the Kerala Armed Police (KAP) battalion, which could take from nine months to three years. This is followed by another tough stint at one of the Armed Reserve Camps (ARCs), with a transfer likely to other ARCs every three years. It is only after this phase is completed that a police constable can exercise any choice in his or her posting. Of course, by then the majority are well into their forties, with their best years behind them.

The tensions inherent in a job that involves such strenuous training and entails confronting situations of conflict and violence often get transferred to the family members of the constables, especially their wives. Said Simi Prabhash, 35, "When I got married, my husband was undergoing his training at the KAP battalion in Thrissur. He would come home just twice every month." Once he moved to the ARC in Kottayam, his home town, Simi moved into her mother-in-law's home in order to meet her husband thrice a week. It's only in the past five years that Simi, her husband, and their two children have been able to live together as a family in Kottayam. Their dingy two-room police lodging has a kitchen, a bedroom, and a tiny toilet. The bed serves as dining table, study table, and ironing board. In all probability, this will be their only permanent home.

Sreeja Ravindran, 35, who is married to a constable based in Thrissur, recalled the first time her husband, Ravindran, left for his training at the KAP battalion in Thrissur: "It was barely three weeks after our marriage. I was nineteen-years-old and all alone in his home at Alleppey. He was soon made the platoon leader of his team and was granted a day off every month. His journey home would take twelve hours and he would end up spending just three or four hours with us, mostly in the wee hours of the night, and then he'd board the bus back to Thrissur."

It is Sreeja's belief that the life of a police constable's wife is almost as tough as that of her husband, given the uncertainties and stress that mark it. This is why she gets furious when she sees films that portray police constables in a poor light. "In movies, they [constables] are depicted either as buffoons or as corrupt criminals. Why doesn't anyone care to find out more about the struggles we face?" she asked angrily.

Both Prabhash and Ravindran, now in their forties, have been police constables for the past fifteen years, working an 8 a.m. to 8 p.m. shift. They do night shifts too, from 8 p.m. to 2 a.m. Prabhash commutes to work on his motorbike and makes sure that he has his lunch at home. Ravindran prefers to take the city bus and settles for a hotel meal for lunch. Neither gets a fuel allowance nor meal reimbursements. All they can afford is to carry a bottle of water with them.

Although every constable is entitled to a day off in a week, it is rarely granted as the ratio of policemen to citizens in Kerala is 1 to 1,000, as opposed to the stipulated 1 to 500. But they earn an additional Rs 150-200 if they work on an off-day, and this is a bonus they can ill-afford to lose, given their modest monthly salary of Rs 10,000 (in 2011).

The situation at home is no better. The biggest problem of this job is the difficulty in obtaining leave. And so, most often, police constables cannot be counted on to be around in times of domestic crises. Women like Sreeja, Simi, and Deepa Prasannan, 37, have had to fend for themselves whenever their children suddenly fell ill and needed to be admitted into a hospital or when a sudden death occurred in the family. Because one parent keeps such irregular hours, the wives of police constables rarely seek employment outside the home.

Although Deepa lives in quarters that look slightly better than those of the others, and her husband, M.K. Prasannan, 42, works as police constable in a police station close by, she doesn't think she is privileged in any way. "My husband works as a paaravu [constable who stands guard at the police station]] from 7 a.m. to 2 p.m. He has night duty thrice a week: it is either bike patrol from 4 p.m. to 5 a.m. or jeep patrol from 11 p.m. to 5 a.m. He doesn't get any time with the family," she says. Prasannan served at the ARC in Thrissur for seven years, then for three years in Idukki, followed by one year at the ARC in Kottayam, before settling down as local constable at the Kottayam East police station for the past six years.

"This may be a good job in terms of honour and security of tenure, but it is impossible for the family of a police constable to save, let alone build a house," revealed Deepa. But more than money, it is the personal security of their husbands that most worries these wives. They are clearly the most vulnerable in a situation of conflict or violence. They are exposed to physical assault, disallowed to react at will, and easily fall prey to ill health. For instance, on days when a VIP makes a visit to the area, constables have to stand in the sun for hours on end. "The trauma I go through each time my husband is called away to places of unrest is difficult to express. Now even my children have stopped asking me why their father has not yet come home," said Sreeja.

As work and family conditions impact adversely on the attitudes and behaviour of the police force, the authorities have been forced to envisage reform measures. In 2011, when we spoke with Premji K. Nair, district president of the Kerala Police Association, which represents police constables and head constables, he spoke of the change in designations: "From 2010, the 'police constable' has become 'civil police officer' and the term 'head constable' has given away to 'senior civil police officer'."

The government has also decided to cut down on the time spent in training at various ARCs and is beginning to assign local postings according to individual choice as soon as new recruits complete their KAP battalion training. This means new recruits could be living in police lodgings with their families in less than two years of joining the force. Earlier, postings at 'mother-stations' – stations at a recruit's or their spouse's home town – were deliberately denied. Now, the department believes that a recruit is most suited to a posting in a place with which he or she is familiar, because the constable will have first-hand knowledge of the area, a wide social network, and could make a smoother transition to post-retirement life.

The idea is to train police personnel who are 'civic-minded' rather than 'force-oriented', so that constables – who are deemed to be the backbone of the police force – conduct themselves in a more enlightened, more citizen-friendly, and less violent manner.

The Lost Daughters of Bengal's Border Communities

Swapna Majumdar

North 24 Parganas (West Bengal): It's not uncommon for young girls to 'vanish' or 'go missing after marriage' or 'get lost' in the villages of the North 24 Parganas and Nadia districts of West Bengal, which straddle the 2,000-kilometre-long India-Bangladesh border.

In July 2010, Shikha Mondal, 16, went missing from her marital home in Tangra village in the Bongaon block of the North 24 Parganas district. One month after she had disappeared, when neighbours inquired after Shikha, they were told that she had got lost while grazing cattle. Then there is the case of Belika Khatun, 15, of Mahakhola village in Nadia district. She was sent with her aunt to get married to a 'good boy' in Delhi three years ago. Since then, her parents, who are daily wage labourers, have not heard from her.

According to West Bengal's Criminal Investigation Department, the number of missing children from the state had increased from 4,621 in 2008 to 8,598 in 2010, and the districts of North 24 Parganas and Nadia report the highest numbers of such missing persons. These borders areas are presumed to be guarded by the Border Security Force (BSF) on the Indian side of the border and the Bangladesh Rifles (BDR) on the other side. Yet, the presence of security forces has not brought a sense of security to the lives of people living in these areas, partly because of the impunity that marks their conduct.

Local people speak of being subject to verbal abuse, intimidation, beatings, and even torture, on the suspicion that they are illegal migrants. In fact, the Banglar Manabadhikar Suraksha Mancha (MASUM), a non-governmental organisation based in Kolkata, has documented over sixty-one killings along the border by the BSF since 2007. According to MASUM, the rights of border communities are constantly being violated.

Security forces regularly storm people's homes and harass them on the pretext of conducting searches for illegal migrants.

The 2010 District Human Development Report of North 24 Parganas, conducted by district authorities, revealed that it is women who are most vulnerable in such circumstances. Their situation is made worse by the prevailing food scarcity and gender unequal social norms. Poverty, poor education, the lack of livelihood opportunities, and abysmal health care result in lives of absolute vulnerability, with women and girls often falling easy victims to human traffickers.

Little did Rinku Mondal, 16, know what she was getting into when she left her border village of Boaldah, in the Bongaon block of the North 24 Parganas, in the hope of augmenting her family's meagre income. All she wanted to do was earn enough to enable her two younger brothers to study. The second of four siblings, Rinku dropped out of school when she was ten to help her mother roll beedis (local cigarettes). It was after four years of living a hand-to-mouth existence that she decided to accompany her neighbour's daughter to Mumbai, despite her parents' opposition.

Rinku's mother, Rekha, was never in favour of sending her daughter to the big city. "I told her not to go, that we would manage with the money that we were earning. I warned her that Mumbai was not a good place and bad things happened to girls there. But she didn't listen to me and quietly left," she recalled.

Rinku returned home some months later wearing sindoor (the vermilion powder worn by Hindu women in the parting of their hair to symbolise marriage). She claimed that she was working in a Mumbai home and had married the man who had got her the job. Although her family was angry with her, they were relieved to see her and pleaded with her to bring her husband and stay back at home. Rinku, however, soon returned to Mumbai. "I begged her not to go, but she said she had to earn more money so that we could lead a better life. When she gave me Rs 9,000, I knew something was wrong," said a clearly distraught Rekha.

Her worst fears came true when Rinku called her in 2010 to say that she had been caught in a police raid and had been sent to a shelter home run by an organisation in Mumbai. Since then, Rekha has been trying to secure her daughter's release, with the help of the Charuigachhi Light House Society (CLHS), a community-based organisation working on child protection issues in the Bongaon block of the North 24 Parganas.

A survey conducted by the National Commission for Women in 2009 revealed that trafficking of women and children for commercial sex was taking place in 378 districts of India – accounting for roughly 62 per cent of the total number of Indian districts. Given its porous border regions, West Bengal has emerged as a prime site for such trafficking.

"There is a demand for young girls by those running prostitution rackets and, going by the numbers rescued from the red-light areas of Mumbai, Pune, and Delhi, the situation is alarming. In 2009, Rescue Foundation, an NGO in Mumbai, helped 176 girls to escape from a red-light area in the city. The youngest of them were girls aged sixteen," said Roop Sen of Sanjog, a Kolkata-based resource organisation working on anti-trafficking and child rights issues.

Evidence-based research into sex trafficking of girls in West Bengal – commissioned by Sanjog in 2010 – reiterated that in situations of stark poverty, it is obvious that local girls will search for better livelihood opportunities. According to Paramita Banerjee, who anchored the study, adolescent girls desire a life different from the one they have experienced. "It is to escape semi-starvation, multiple pregnancies, and domestic violence that they succumb to inducements like income-earning opportunities outside their villages," she explained. Most often, these girls end up in brothels across India, with the most likely destination being Mumbai. However, according to Sen, since sexual exploitation is no longer confined just to brothels, tracing and rescuing the girls has become extremely difficult.

Sanjog, which is using its knowledge and resources to

strengthen and sustain efforts to address trafficking and exploitation of adolescents and children, has teamed up with several community-based organisations, like CLHS. One such initiative focuses on reducing the prevalence of early marriage of girls in these districts – a major factor that facilitates trafficking. Cross-border tensions and uncertainty mean that education is almost certainly disrupted. This, in turn, has serious consequences – like early marriage. According to government figures, over 80 per cent of the children in rural North 24 Parganas are married before they turn adults. This not only impacts negatively on their physical health and mental development, it has consequences for their future security as well. That is why CLHS is working to stop local communities from marrying off their daughters before they turn eighteen. "Families are not keen on educating their children, particularly their daughters. Poverty drives them to marry them young because then they do not have to pay dowries or feed them. They don't realise that their daughters are at risk of being trafficked in the process," said Palash Roy, CLHS's founder.

The Sanjog study also showed that the chances of daughters marrying young are higher in female-headed households, and it is precisely these families who lose their daughters to trafficking.

The West Bengal state government has attempted remedial measures. But their impact has been insignificant, largely because of the lack of political will and the fact that the various implementing bodies have failed to work together. Meanwhile, communities living near the border continue to lose their daughters to forces far beyond their control.

When Sikkim Shook

Saadia Azim

Gangtok (Sikkim): When an earthquake measuring 6.9 on

the Richter scale struck the tiny north-eastern state of Sikkim in September 2011, Kima Sherpa, 56, who was living on the outer verandah of Vijra cinema hall in state capital Gangtok, did not leave her temporary shelter for fear of losing all her hard-earned belongings.

Just six months earlier, Kima and her husband, a carpenter, had left their home in Lingtam village in eastern Sikkim, in the hope of making more prosperous lives for themselves in the city. That move proved to be a disastrous mistake in the wake of the earthquake. Even as her husband urged her to run for cover while the walls around them were crumbling, a part of the roof of the hall suddenly came crashing down upon her. Kima was rescued from the rubble with deep cuts on her head and face and was rushed to a local hospital. Later, when she regained consciousness, she found that her right leg had been amputated.

A month later, as Kima lay helplessly on her hospital bed, the traumatised woman revealed, "Our family has a small farm in Lingtam. It's just my husband and I, along with my brother-in-law, his wife, and their daughter. In the village, my brother-in-law's family sold farm produce to run their home and we hardly had any money. That's why we came here."

When Kima lost her leg, the cinema hall owner contributed Rs 5,000 for her treatment, which came in handy, but was clearly a pittance. When the government sanctioned Rs 50,000 as compensation to them, Kima and her husband felt a little better. But she knows that life will never again be the same for her and she is "not really sure" if the money she received will cover the expenses of health care in the future.

Of course, life in the immediate future looks very bleak, but Kima is one of the luckier ones: she, at least, is alive, unlike so many others. Being in Gantok, she was able to get timely medical attention. Scores of women, especially the ailing, elderly or pregnant, had to wait for days before a doctor could attend to them. In fact, many of them were transported to Sikkim's capital from distant villages and small towns by rescue teams after being left stranded for days.

Accessing health care has never been easy in a state that already has limited health facilities and support services. Gangtok is really still the only place where hospitals are somewhat geared to handle such emergencies. "We had no option but to ferry the injured to safe places in Gangtok," said Mridula Agarwal, state coordinator for the Helping Hands Group, an umbrella organisation that was formed when various non-governmental organisations got together to work for the rehabilitation of quake victims. "Sikkim, as such, has always remained cut off from the rest of the country, and even within this small state all regions are not easily accessible. When rescuers first came here, they had no clue about how to reach out and attend to the distressed people," she added.

Indeed, Sikkim, the least populous state in India, generally tends to be forgotten by the rest of the country. Most Indians do not even realise that, apart from Gangtok, a major part of Sikkim falls in the extremely difficult terrain of the high Himalayas. Apart from National Highway 31, there are no motorable roads to its interior villages. What made things worse during the rescue efforts were the landslides everywhere, caused not just by the earthquake, but also by the inclement weather that followed the calamity.

Nerkit Lepcha, 31, can vouch for the rough conditions that women like her have had to face while negotiating the inaccessible terrain. The stress she experienced after the quake drove her into premature labour, but there was no one to help her out. It was some time before an army team could airlift her from the sleepy village of Chungthang in north Sikkim and get her to STNM Hospital in Gangtok. She gave birth to a baby girl minutes after she was admitted. "Had relief not reached me on time it would not have been easy," she confessed, adding, "We still do not know what happened to others like me who could not be rescued in time."

For people living in remote locations in Sikkim, modern medical assistance is a rare luxury. Most tend to take recourse to local home-made remedies or visit monasteries for medical help. Said Bishal Cintury, a volunteer from Gangtok who works with monasteries in north Sikkim to raise social awareness among the people, "The quake came as a real eye-opener to us in terms of showing up the inadequacy of our health care system. The main reason for this is the fact that large parts of Sikkim are still unconnected with the rest of India and people shy away from approaching the few government-aided programmes that do exist because of unfamiliarity."

While the chaos, devastation, and deprivation have been particularly tough on women and children, some modest efforts to ease their situation must be flagged. For instance, female army pilots were included during helicopter rescue sorties to facilitate the evacuation of women, especially those who were pregnant. In fact, in one single endeavour, four women who were in labour were airlifted from north Sikkim and brought to Gangtok in time – Nerkit being one of them.

Every earthquake comes as a reality check on the standards of life of people, and the Sikkim earthquake was no exception. Millions the world over have been exposed to a quake's devastating effects and, according to sources like *The Lancet*, nearly 60 per cent of all disaster-related mortality can be traced to the natural calamity. Its impacts are not just immediate, but long-term. Those surviving crush injuries, like Kima Sherpa, for instance, are left to face a future marked by serious physical disability. It becomes important, therefore, to remain engaged with the task of rehabilitation and recovery long after the incident itself.

Manita Pradhan, Secretary, Sikkim's Women and Child Welfare Division, has agreed with this assessment and reiterated the need for continued focus on the state's health care delivery in the months and years to come, especially among women who, in any case, lead very difficult lives.

But Srijana, who comes from the village of Lumsey, on the outskirts of Gangtok, which was not as badly affected as the rest of the state, is worried that Sikkim, along with the earthquake that shook it, will soon be treated as a footnote in the annals of India's history. "This state has always been left out. The earthquake came as a reminder of how much we lack in health care systems here. This time we must make sure that the promises made in the aftermath of the earthquake to Sikkim are kept by New Delhi," she said.

Mumbai Blasts: Emergency Response Lost in Transportation

Geeta Seshu

Mumbai (Maharashtra): A riveting photograph of the bomb blasts that shook Mumbai in July 2011 was of bloodied victims being transported in a tempo to the nearest hospital – a telling comment on the state of emergency care in a city that has faced major terror attacks every few years and, given its very large population, has scores of minor emergencies every day.

Mumbai is no stranger to emergencies. There were the 1992-93 riots (900 casualties), the serial blasts of 1993 (250 dead), the bomb blasts of 2003 (54 dead), the floods of 2005 (447 dead), the train blasts of 2006 (200 casualties), the terror attacks of November 26, 2008 (200 dead), and the three blasts of 2011 that claimed 26 lives. Yet, even today, preparedness is the last thing the average city dweller can hope to experience.

Consider this: following the 2011 blasts, Maharashtra Chief Minister Prithviraj Chauhan went on record to state that he was not able to get in touch with his colleagues for fifteen minutes because the telephone lines were down. And, according to eyewitness R.C. Shah, a trader at the Dadar blast site near Kabutarkhana, the police arrived fifteen minutes late, ambulances were unavailable, and the injured were ferried to hospitals in taxis and tempos.

Incensed by the images of victims being transported in a tempo, Dr. Sanjay Nagral, a senior surgeon who operates at the city's premier Jaslok Hospital, penned an anguished article in a local daily. According to him, the world over, emergency care follows the concept of the 'golden hour' and transport is an essential aspect of this response. "This is not the first time we have voiced the need for specialised emergency care. But it has not been a priority," commented Dr. Nagral.

During an emergency, he elaborated, triage – the task of categorising those affected into fatalities, the most severely injured, and the less severely injured – is absolutely vital. Transporting victims in well-equipped ambulances that are staffed by trained paramedics is the next step. A proper mode of transport is important in case a patient may have suffered a spinal injury, Dr. Nagral pointed out. But are these standard procedures being followed in India?

If a victim survives the breakdown of emergency procedures or the lack of proper ambulance services, what does the system have to offer in terms of trauma care? The Mumbai blasts of July 2011 demonstrated that the options were clearly limited. There was the civic administration-run Sion Hospital in south-central Mumbai. But this twenty-five-year-old, fifteen-bed centre was not only overburdened – since it also catered to victims of road accidents on the Mumbai-Pune highway – it was also in desperate need of an overhaul.

Another trauma centre at the government-run J.J. Hospital in south Mumbai hadn't been set up then, despite sanctioned approval at a cost of around Rs 40 crores. Said Dr. T.P. Lahane, dean of J.J. Hospital, "We have everything ready for the centre. It will be equipped with trained personnel – ward boys, nurses, technicians, doctors, investigation facilities, MRI or CT scans – everything will function like a self-sufficient division."

Despite the absence of a specialised trauma care centre, Dr. Lahane averred that J.J. Hospital was able to provide the twenty-five patients sent there during the 2011 blasts with immediate care within the golden hour. "We got information of the blasts by 7:10 p.m. and by 7:30, around 200 medical personnel, including 35 doctors, were waiting in the lobby. The first patient arrived at 8:10 p.m. From then, our operation theatre worked till 1:30 p.m., until the next team took over," he said. He added that it wasn't just the golden hour, but the forty-six hours that follow that are crucial. Increasing the capacity of the current 20-bed disaster ward to 100 beds and doubling the 4 operating theatres would have definitely helped improve patient care, he felt.

Of course, emergency does not always strike in the form of extreme violence. Mumbai has also had to contend with natural disasters like floods, which have brought the city to its knees in the past few years. Today, there is a 108 helpline that connects to the Disaster Management Department of the Municipal Corporation of Greater Mumbai, the apex civic body that administers the city. This was set up after the 2006 floods and a major part of its work is to monitor the flood situation, says a senior official of the department, who did not wish to be named. "We have thirty-five automatic rain gauges that are updated every fifteen minutes and they give us data on the rainfall across the city. Low-lying areas are particularly monitored," he added.

The personnel in this unit have been trained to deal with all kinds of emergency situations, including fire-fighting, rescue, flood relief, and wall collapses. The helpline gets at least 100 calls a day, but even the helpline staff felt that there is a need for better ambulances and trained paramedics. "Many deaths are due to faulty transport to hospitals and we must have special ambulances. We also need better civic and traffic sense from the public. Often, ambulances don't get right-of-way," the civic official rued.

In the absence of trained personnel and in light of tawdry service, it's caring and responsive Mumbaikers who have always come to the rescue – such as Sanjay Bengali, proprietor of a printing press, who lives on the second floor of a building opposite the Kabutarkhana area of Dadar in central Mumbai, one of the recent blast sites. He recalled, "At first, I thought the noise was of a tube light bursting in the advertising hoarding on the bus shelter. But when we saw the thick smoke rise up, we realised it was something worse." When the smoke began to clear, Bengali saw two bodies – a woman and a man – lying on the road. Calling out to his son to help, he rushed downstairs. Initially, the two saw the woman moaning and bleeding, while the man seemed still. But then he, too, began to stir. Bengali and his son immediately stopped a passing taxi, picked up the man, and put him into the cab. Meanwhile, others helped the woman by requisitioning a passing police van to take her to the hospital.

Bengali and his wife, Nisha, felt that people should always come forward during an emergency. "We mustn't panic, and when the police come, we must help them in their work instead of crowding the site," the duo observed. However, when they were told that, according to emergency response guidelines, patients must not be picked up until an ambulance arrives, Bengali said, "When we see someone bleeding, what must we do? If we get the person to a hospital quickly, maybe his life can be saved. Besides, we took care to pick up this man carefully."

J.J. Hospital's Dr. Lahane agreed with the Bengalis' approach: "The type of vehicle the patient comes in is not important, the speed with which they come is. I don't think they will get a fracture or anything if they are not transported in the right vehicle. They are, in any case, in deep shock and the protective response of their body makes them rigid. We need to respond in the best way we can."

Given the overstretched public services, private initiatives in emergency care have emerged – although they are expensive. Ziqitza Health Care Ltd. has a thirty-ambulance service that is fully equipped with cardiac equipment, mobile intensive care units, and GPS. The company has also partnered with the state governments of Kerala, Bihar, and Punjab.

But, for Dr. Lahane, there were no short cuts. He believed that it was the responsibility of the government to spend wisely the money allocated to the public health care system, which was invariably tested in traumatic times, such as when blasts rip through a city leaving death and injury in their wake.

Survival Guides

"...women are not helpless instruments to be used by men."

In the Valley, Women Paramedics with a Healing Touch

Aditi Bhaduri

Budgam (Jammu & Kashmir): It was just another mundane day for Munira Manzoor until a knock on the door changed her life. That moment marked her journey of transformation: from being a school drop-out, she became a respected paramedic in her village of Zuhama, in Kashmir's Budgam district.

The year was 1997. The Valley was in the throes of armed insurgency and the health care system, especially in the remote areas of the state of Jammu and Kashmir, was in a shambles. "Most of the doctors, who were from the minority Hindu community, had fled Kashmir, and both the government and private health care facilities were in a poor state. Even the treatment of small injuries was not possible since the paramedics were too scared to step out of their homes. This severely affected women, particularly pregnant women. The nearest maternity home was at Lal Ded Hospital, Srinagar, and for people in remote villages, it took an impossibly long time to reach the hospital since they had to stop at army check posts every now and then," recalled Munira, who is in her mid-thirties.

This crisis in health care deeply disturbed Dr. Ali Mohamed Mir, a retired IAS officer. He wanted to do something about it. So he collaborated with the J&K Voluntary Health and Development Association (J&K VHDA) and decided to reach out to the villages most deprived of health care. Ten villages in Budgam, seven in Pulwama and five in Khansaab, a block near the border, were adopted.

In the beginning, the J&K VHDA organised outpatient departments (OPDs) for administering first aid. But it was observed that women were very reluctant to get treated by male doctors and paramedics. That is when it was decided that if the basic health care needs of the women of the Valley were to be met in some small measure, a team of local women paramedics needed to be set up. That was how Mir found himself going from door-to-door in these villages, asking women and girls to volunteer; and that was how Munira suddenly found herself undergoing training in basic health care, natal care, and later, even in post-trauma counselling.

While the J&K VHDA conducted OPDs, they simultaneously trained the volunteers. As a Class IX drop-out, Munira had never thought that she would one day be able to make such a valuable contribution to her community, but when Mir presented her with the opportunity, she instantly agreed to join up. "I learnt about antenatal and postnatal care. I underwent training gradually, and began by going from home to home to register pregnant women," she recalled. She was also taught how to talk to women about basic health care, nutrition, and even trimester care.

All this was not easy to do under the shadow of militancy. Munira undertook this work at great personal risk – as did Haseena Begum and, later, Sakeena Shafi, Safeena, and many others. According to these women, although they felt insecure, they were able to undergo training and help local women because caregiving was regarded as non-political work. Mir's daughter, Ezabar Ali, who conducted the training sessions, observed, "To make our working transparent, we conducted all our meetings in the open so that the entire village would know what the volunteers were doing."

Yet, despite the open attitude adopted by Ezabar and her team, as well as the volunteers, they faced a lot of opposition, and even ridicule, when the time came to step into the homes of friends and neighbours. Recalled Sakeena Shafi of Gundi Maqsood village, "Initially, people laughed at me. They would poke fun, saying, 'Look, the doctor has come'." She had just passed Class X when she attended her first J&K VHDA medical camp and decided to undergo training as a paramedic. Her family was supportive and she finally became a volunteer in

1999. At first, it hurt when people mocked her, but Sakeena stood firm and attitudes gradually began to change as people understood the benefits of such an intervention.

Eventually, Sakeena became indispensable for the pregnant women in her village and an expert advisor when it came to antenatal and postnatal care. She also talked to local women about family planning and occasionally helped train other volunteers as well. Dais (traditional birth attendants) were one such category of volunteers who received training in basic hygiene – like using hot water and clean sheets while delivering babies. The use of medical kits was also explained to them.

Safeena, a volunteer from Zuhama village, was also thrilled at getting the opportunity to help her people. Inspired by Munira to undergo training, she proved particularly effective in reaching out to emotionally disturbed women, some on the brink of a nervous breakdown.

Owing to the decades of violence, trauma counselling and mental health care have emerged as huge concerns in Kashmir. Scores of mothers whose sons disappeared or were killed by the militants or security agencies have suffered immeasurable distress. Wives have had husbands remain untraceable for years and find themselves trying to cope with the pressures of loneliness and uncertainty every moment of their lives. Today, although the level of violence has come down, unemployment and other social problems have given rise to high levels of domestic violence and this, in turn, is a significant factor in undermining the mental well-being of women and children.

Many women in far-flung villages have had to suffer domestic violence in silence for years. But now, in volunteer-counsellors like Safeena, they find a sympathetic ear. For instance, Magli, 70, who lost a young son to militants and suffered from acute depression, found someone with whom she could converse when Safeena started visiting her regularly. Although Magli initially resisted the idea of talking to a stranger, she gradually opened up. Safeena also advised her on taking some simple medication for her insomnia and Magli slowly began to recover some of her old composure.

While local women have benefited from these enterprising volunteers, the volunteers too have gained greatly from the experience. Besides the increased confidence and respect they now command within their own homes and communities, Munira pointed out that she and her colleagues are also more aware of women's health needs as well as their rights. "We had no idea about immunisation and we learnt of its importance during the training. Young girls reach puberty here with little inkling about personal hygiene. Once we counselled them, the situation improved. After all, even as mothers we did not earlier have a sense of the changes our bodies undergo and the care we need to take," she elaborated.

Understanding domestic violence also proved to be an eye-opener. The rise of domestic violence has been specifically connected to the series of hartals and bandhs (shut-downs) Kashmir has been witnessing. Since most of these bandhs are called by separatists who are accountable to no one, people are too afraid to oppose them. "Hartals lead to loss of wages and many of our men are daily wage earners," revealed Munira. According to her, such situations only increase the frustration of local men and they give vent to it by attacking their wives and, sometimes, their children. Sometimes, Munira has had to intervene personally and rescue those who had no idea about how to deal with such displays of anger and bitterness from close family members.

In 2011, there were over fifty active women health volunteers in Budgam, Pulwama, Baramullah, and Srinagar. Besides the health care they deliver, they have emerged as icons for the local people. They have also had the unexpected effect of raising the status of the girl child. "Earlier, most families sent only their sons to school. But after seeing our work, they are paying attention to their daughters. They can see that girls too can play a role in the development of families and the community," explained Safeena.

6,300 ft above Sea Level, a Kashmir School Helps Girls Reach for the Sky

Anjali Singh

Rajouri (Jammu & Kashmir): Nestled 6,300 feet above sea level, surrounded by dense forests, is Govind High School of Pichnar village near Kotranka town, which is about sixty kilometres northeast of Rajouri district in Jammu & Kashmir. It is a unique institution located in a troubled region, and testifies to the principle that no matter the situation, no matter the conflict, local children must be allowed to access education to ensure their health and well-being.

Rajouri has been the site of insurgency for decades. But tucked away in its isolated location, Govind High School carries on with its mandate of providing good education to local children, especially girls, and has emerged as one of the most popular educational institutions in the region.

Both the school administration and students have learnt to take the spectre of violence in their stride. During our visit to the school in 2011, Afzal Mohammed, the headmaster, said, "The school stands close to an army chowki (army post), yet the students are not affected by the threat of violence. They are more focused on building a future for themselves. I have not seen any student terrified of coming to school for fear of terror attacks. Even demonstrations and agitations in places like Srinagar have had no impact here. Since we are situated in such a remote area, information related to the conflict hardly trickles down to us."

A significant aspect of this institution is that it has over 200 students, but what makes it even more special is that more than half of each class comprises girls, who come from the villages that surround Kotranka town. It takes two hours or more of non-stop walking for some of them to reach the school, but fuelled by their dreams, these young women put up with the tough terrain and inclement weather to clock in at 10 a.m. every school day.

What came as a pleasant surprise to Mohammed when he became headmaster in May 2010 was to find that nobody complained about the lack of facilities, least of all the students. When he got to know them better, he was touched to hear stories about how most of them – especially the girls – travelled such long distances to school without a murmur.

Talking to the students confirmed the headmaster's observations. Said Zarina Begum, 15, from Kha village, who was studying in Class X, "We just love school, because it brings the wider world to us. Education is the only way girls can experience change. I want to be a teacher so that I can help other girls step out of their homes. We live in such a remote place that it takes me two to three hours to reach school, but I come with a few other girls from my village. We walk as a group for safety's sake."

One of the younger among five siblings, Zarina's intelligence was clearly discernible. When asked whether she would be able to stand up to a male-dominated society, she replied quickly, "Ladkon ke saath mil ke desh ke liye kaam karenge, aur accha naam karenge." (We will work together with the boys for the good of the country and make our village proud.)

Shakuntala Devi, 14, from Kanthol village, who was in Class IX, believed that she was particularly lucky and went on to explain why: "I am the first of the daughters in my family to come to a school. Luckily, my parents agreed to send me to this school though it is so far away. My three elder sisters were not allowed to come, so I know how important this education is for me." Did it not bother her that she had to wake up early every day and trudge for two hours, crossing jungles and bad roads, to reach school? "No. I love to study science, which is being taught here. So I come to school however long it may take me. I want to be a doctor," revealed the youngster.

With religious fundamentalists coming down hard on educating girls in Kashmir, one would have imagined that these girls would be apprehensive about schooling. But retorted Shakuntala, "We have no electricity, no proper roads, no system of health care and no clean drinking water. I think these problems are far bigger for us than the diktat of militants."

Truly, these girls came across as determined youngsters endowed with a strong will to rise above their circumstances. Their life is certainly no easy ride. Most villages in this region have no electricity or proper civic amenities, and the families are generally large, with eight or nine children. Given the number of hungry mouths to feed, education is a luxury for most households. Girls, especially, have a rough time because many families believe that the more hands there are to keep the home running, the better. Early marriage is also the practice here, with many women having their first child in their teens.

Given this scenario, the importance of a school like Govind High School is obvious. If it had not existed, life would have been very different for many of its young students. The school has ensured that the fundamental right to education is upheld, even under inhospitable circumstances.

Said Afzal Mohammed, "These children have the zeal to make something out of life and I realised that it was a privilege to be able to teach them. They taught me that it is a teacher who has the power to help realise a child's dream of becoming a doctor, engineer, pilot or soldier. So I decided to make sure that I would try my best to ensure that these children get the facilities to study better."

The principal was well aware that the facilities at the institution were in need of an upgrade. "When I took over, I was taken aback to see that the school was functioning with only five staff members as against the required strength of twenty. There was also a dearth of buildings to house the classes properly," he said. According to Mohammed's assessment, the complex needed at least seven more buildings if it was to function properly, and making the right improvements was very much in the sights of the principal and his five colleagues. The school had no science lab, playgrounds or even library. Many posts of Class IV employees (tertiary staff) were lying vacant. But things had started changing in 2011. Said the principal, "After we met education officials and described the poor state of the school, we got one more building under the Sarva Shiksha Abhiyan, taking the total count up to four. Even the 60th Rashtriya Rifles, posted at Rajouri, pitched in with furniture and sports equipment, thanks to some helpful officers. So things are beginning to look up."

What remains the biggest challenge, however, is ensuring that the girls of Class X get to take their Higher Secondary Board Examinations every year. This is a hurdle that entails travelling a distance of thirty to thirty-five kilometres to reach Dangri, a town even farther than Rajouri, where the examination centres are located. Yet, each year they have managed to make sure that no student misses an examination, according to seventeen-year-old Mohammed Bashir, who had himself passed out of this school and now keenly watches his nine-year-old sister make her way through it.

Bashir is a wise young man who has realised how important schooling for girls is in this remote region. He firmly stated, "It is only when girls are educated that our village can find a place for itself in the world. So girls here have to go and take their examinations, even if they have to change three buses to reach the centre. There are many hardships we face in the villages, especially when someone falls ill. The nearest hospital is miles away. So if our sisters can study and become doctors and teachers, it will only help the rest of us."

Azamgarh's Women Fight Stigma and Stereotypes

Kulsum Mustafa

Azamgarh (Uttar Pradesh): The village of Sanjarpur in the Azamgarh district of Uttar Pradesh has had a terror tag attached to it ever since the police encounter that took place in Batla House in Delhi's Jamia Nagar, on September 19, 2008. Atif Amin, one of the two young men killed in that encounter, was from this village, as was Ariz Khan, picked up by the police after the encounter. Several other youth on the police's 'Wanted' list are from this village too.

A visit to Sanjarpur, a year and eight months after the Batla House encounter, revealed how deeply the incident had impacted life here. The women of Sanjarpur had not celebrated any festival since then; neither had they taken the same pleasure in dressing up or applying henna on their hands and feet, as they had earlier. When they spoke about their lives, they expressed only one desire: to get justice for their children, restore peace and bring tranquility back into "hearts and hearths".

While adversity had devastated them, it was apparent that, in a way, it had also helped these pardanashin (veiled) women – most of them illiterate – to rediscover their inner strength. The spirit to fight back against what they termed an "injustice", an attempt to malign their community and, above all, a planned strategy to prevent the progress of their children, was very evident, even as they unanimously condemned terrorist acts.

While the men in the village had stepped back, intimidated by the security forces, local women emerged as the emotional bedrock of their families. Adopting a two-pronged strategy, they were working towards bringing some normalcy back into their homes at the same time as trying to gain more information about the law through legal awareness sessions conducted by the Association for Advocacy and Legal Initiative (AALI), a Lucknow-based non-governmental organisation which came to Sanjarpur at the initiative of Tariq Saif, a local social activist.

AALI had decided to fight the criminal cases of the Sanjarpur youth and also empower community women by holding exclusive all-women monthly sessions on law and human rights in the village. Elaborating on their work in Sanjarpur, Shubi Dwividi, a programme officer at AALI, said, "We advocate and work for issues and concerns of women, especially those involving minority and deprived communities." According to her, AALI had developed strategies to support the Muslim community in Sanjarpur to stand up against state oppression and social defamation. "We want to ensure that guilt is not established at the cost of the innocent," she said.

Needless to say, this was a principle this eastern Uttar Pradesh village wanted to establish, and no one was more conscious of the need to do so than its women. "By ensuring that the food is cooked, the house is cleaned and clothes are washed we do try to pretend that everything is fine. But we know this is not enough. We need legal know-how," said Rahat, an aunt of Arif, a suspected terrorist currently lodged in a Gujarat prison.

Rahat, a divorcée in her mid-thirties and a victim of domestic violence, may have had severe hearing impairment and a loss of 70 per cent of her vision, but she said her physical disabilities would never come in the way of her fight for justice. In fact, she was one of the most enthusiastic supporters and participants of the legal empowerment initiative.

AALI started work here in November 2008 and quickly made its way into the hearts of local women. Through advocacy, it raised the issue at various levels. It also helped them form defence committees, comprising lawyers and others, to ensure that the rule of law, natural justice and an adequate defence would be made available to them.

"Behind their veils they are all holed up. They need to open up, speak out. This will reduce the pain," remarked Sehba Syed, a former AALI member, who has worked in Sanjarpur. Dwividi agreed with this assessment: "This is very true, which is why we came up with the idea of mental health camps."

A walk through the dusty village lanes only strengthened one's belief that psychiatric support was absolutely vital for these distraught women who refused to believe in the guilt of their relatives. Shamsa, Arif's eldest sister, was convinced that her brother had been framed. "He is innocent and he has been made a scapegoat. How could a boy who could not see a chicken being slaughtered have had a hand in a blast that killed innocent people?" she asked. Arif's mother, Farzana Begum, too, was inconsolable, even though her tears had run dry after weeks of having cried herself to sleep. She sat near the window, head bent, cutting vegetables. Though the black dupatta covering her head partially fell over her face, it failed to hide the deep circles under her eyes and the lines of sorrow that were etched on her face. "After the initial few days of inactivity when she seemed to have lost the will to live, Ammi took stock of herself. Now, she does all the household chores just like before, but that is just a façade. She keeps looking through the window, from where she last bid khuda hafiz (goodbye) to Arif," said Shamsa.

The scene at slain youngster Atif Amin's house was even more heart-rending. An eerie silence hung over the house. It seemed almost like an eternity before the gate was opened and entry inside was allowed most reluctantly. "Ammi is very ill. She has been hospitalised. Only we sisters are at home," said Tabish, Atif's sister, quietly. "Life will never be the same again for us, we can never come to terms with Atif's death. He was the youngest of five siblings, the darling of the family, so helpful, so nice, even to total strangers. He was always helping anyone who was new to Delhi..." Tabish's voice broke off and soon she was sobbing loudly. Beenish, the eldest sister, consoled her, "We will have to learn to live without him. This is our destiny."

The stigma of terror had not only eclipsed the lives of these families but put a blot on the future of the youth growing up to be young men here. Just the mere fact that they hailed from Azamgarh was enough to invite suspicion. While the humiliation of being ostracised chilled their souls, the prospect of a bleak future stared them in the face.

"We have to constantly remind ourselves that this is all a bad dream," said the mother of Yusuf Ali. The software engineer, who worked in Noida, near Delhi, has been rendered jobless because his employer and landlord both showed him the door. His only fault: he was from Azamgarh. Mohammed

Nasir, another software engineer based in Gurgaon, quit his job and went back to tilling his paddy fields. Nasir's frightened parents had urged him to come back home after the Batla House incident.

"Azamgarhis are being thrown out of jobs and accommodation on flimsy grounds," said Tariq, who is fearful that most parents here, out of fear and insecurity, may stop sending their wards out for studies and employment or may, like Nasir's parents, pressurise them to return home. "It took so many years for Muslims here to accept that education is the only way forward for them, the only way of being part of the mainstream, but once again they have been forced to change their minds. This is a grave situation," he commented. Yet, along with a few like-minded youngsters, Tariq made up his mind to fight this trend by motivating women to send their children back to school and out to seek jobs.

Azamgarh needs to re-imagine itself. It needs to be infused with a fresh zeal for life. The task is difficult and requires consistent effort. But women here know that the onus of restoring peace ultimately lies on them. It is they who will ensure whether their community remains in the mainstream or gets pushed to the margins.

One woman from the village described what it felt like: "It's like walking on live coals." But people here also know that what they do today will help put the past behind them and build a future for their children.

Illness and Debility Can't Stop Manipur's Meira Paibis

Anjulika Thingnam

Imphal (Manipur): The ongoing conflict in the north-eastern state of Manipur, that has stretched over six decades, has affected generations of women in many direct and indirect ways. Health has been a natural casualty in this region, where even something as basic as clean drinking water is scarce. In many areas, people use either pond water or river water, neither of which is free from contamination and which perpetuates water-borne diseases. There has also been a substantial increase in malaria cases, said to have risen from 708 in 2008 to 1,069 in 2009: an increase of 51 per cent. Tuberculosis is another widespread problem, and with significant numbers of people living with HIV/AIDS in the state, it is not surprising that the HIV-TB co-infection is also manifesting itself.

According to Dr. M. Akshayakumar Singh, head of the Department of Clinical Psychology at the Regional Institute of Medical Sciences in Imphal, Manipur's state capital, social tensions and violence related to the armed conflict are affecting the average person both mentally and physically. "Fear, anxiety, tension, stress and depression are the most prominent effects seen, manifested physiologically as palpitations, ulcers, colitis, irregular bowel movements, dizziness, headache, backache and many other social diseases such as diabetes," he said.

Those on the frontlines of the struggle for justice in this region have lived with deteriorating health for years. Take the Meira Paibis – 'torch-bearers' – a women's group that has a presence in almost all nine districts of the state. The group is actively engaged in fighting rights violations, whether perpetrated by local people or security personnel.

Phanjoubam Sakhi, 75, one of the pioneering leaders of the Meira Paibis, has worked tirelessly for almost as long as armed conflict has raged in her state. Recalled Sakhi, "I must have been around forty when I first started involving myself in the movement. My youngest child was around thirteen years old then."

The Meira Paibi movement originally began as a nishabandi (prohibition) movement during the 1970s. "At night, I would open the cupboard as casually as possible, stealthily take out the clothes I would wear the next day and keep them by my pillow, to stop my husband from suspecting that I was about to set out early the next morning on Meira Paibi work. On my return, I would peek at the house from the gate and sneak in when he was not around," Sakhi recalled with an impish smile.

The years of work she has put in have earned her the epithet 'Ima' (mother). But being so honoured has come at great personal cost and sacrifice. "We would set out at dawn without food. With the few ten-rupee notes that lay at the bottom of our purses, how could we buy food? At most we could only afford some snacks, but in interior Manipur, even these were not available," Sakhi recounted. Such lives of uncertainty inevitably took a toll on the women's health. "Our circumstances affected our health a lot," said Sakhi, who is the president of the All Manipur Kanba Ima Lup (AMKIL), one of the prominent statewide Meira Paibi organisations.

It's not just Sakhi who is suffering. Most Meira Paibi women complain of gastritis, insomnia, dizzy spells, anxiety and fatigue. "During the peak of agitations, we go to bed, yet lie awake unable to sleep for hours, thinking about what could be the best course of action," Sakhi said, adding humorously, "Sometimes we think about how best to outmanoeuvre the police and stop them from trying to arrest us."

Like Sakhi, Ima Gyaneshori, 60, AMKIL's publicity secretary, has her share of health problems. "I have been a diabetic since 1994, much before I became involved in Meira Paibi work," she said, "so, the frequent irregularity of food intake during the agitations can be very bad for me. Yet, I cannot forego my work as it has become part of my life's purpose." She said she and her colleagues have kept going only by the exercise of sheer will. "We usually derive the strength to go on from within ourselves. But, at times, after a campaign would come to an end, my whole body would ache and I would be bedridden with fatigue and dizziness," she revealed.

Their campaigns are by no means easy. Take the Sharmila Kanba Lup, a support group formed by a few senior Meira Paibis. They take turns in staying overnight in a small lean-to, walled by bamboo mats, on the side of Porompat road in Imphal East district, a few metres away from the state-run J.N. Hospital where Irom Sharmila is being kept under judicial custody and force-fed.

Nongthongbam Nupimacha, 62, of the All Manipur Women Social Reformation and Development Samaj, has observed these vigils very often. When we met her in 2011, she estimated that she may have slept at her own home for just a night or two over the last two years.

Another activist, Ima L. Gyaneshori, 60, said she always carries a pack of biscuits in her bag to counter any fluctuations in her blood sugar levels. She also makes sure that her blood pressure medication is always at hand, a precaution that has become essential ever since she actively participated in the relay hunger strike for Sharmila, who herself has been on an indefinite fast for more than ten years, for the repeal of the controversial Armed Forces Special Powers Act, 1958.

Dizziness and back pain are constant complaints for Ima Soibam Momon, 67. President of the All Manipur Tammi Chingmi Apunba Nupi Lup, another prominent Meira Paibi organisation, Momon has developed some indigenous healing techniques to overcome them. "We have so many health complaints, so we burn incense, pray, and apply aloe vera pulp on our heads. Yoga also helps," she averred.

Grace Shatsang, 59, former president of the Naga Women's Union, Manipur, and presently on its advisory committee, believed that the impact of her work as a peace-builder is more dependent on her mental rather than physical health, "My work involves a lot of travelling and constant brainstorming, but it is the psychological stress that is wearing me down." Shatsang hasn't had a health check-up in over three years because there just hasn't been any time.

Agitations and protest movements are everyday occurrences in Manipur given the high levels of violence in the state. According to media reports, in 2009, as many as 235 people were killed between January and April alone. There have been times when years of pent-up tension, frustration, and fury has manifested in raw emotion. The nude protest by twelve Meira Paibi women in 2004, against the extra-judicial rape and killing by Assam Rifles personnel of Thangjam Manorama, a young woman alleged to be a member of an underground group, was one such moment. Explained Dr. Singh, "Exposing their naked bodies in front of the Kangla Fort was the culmination of days of mental disquiet. Tensions ran so high that they did something that was beyond all thought."

Lourembam Nganbi, 60, vice-president of the Bishnupur district unit of AMKIL, recalled that moment: "We gathered at the gate, spread out the banners, and then swiftly shed our clothes. We could not hear or see anything else except our furious voices. We were in a trance-like state." She, along with Momon and Gyaneshori, were among the twelve mothers who had participated in that protest.

The impact of conflict on the health of peace-builders and human rights activists is rarely highlighted, much less understood. But, going by the accounts of the Meira Paibi women, its impacts are deep and long-lasting.

Fighting for Gender Rights in Manipur's Centre of Violence

Ninglun Hanghal

Churachandpur (Manipur): Manipur is no different from the usual conflict zone where it is women who bear the brunt of chaos and bloodshed. While Manipuri women have been at the receiving end of pain and suffering for years now, they have also learnt to come together against all violence, whether triggered by the state's security forces or by militant groups. While the work of women's organisations like the Imphal-based Meira Paibis is well known, there are many small local organisations in other parts of the state that are also responding with courage.

One of these is the Hmar Women's Association (HWA), a group formed by women of the Hmar tribal community, in Lamka, the headquarters of Churachandpur district. In the many years that it has been working to fight atrocities against women, the year 2006 was a watershed. When its members learnt from media reports in early 2006 that around twenty-five women – many of them still in their teens – had been tortured, molested, and sexually harassed by so-called 'underground outfits' in villages like Parbung, Hmarkhawpui, and Sipuikawn, they knew that they had to fight back.

These villages are located in the Tipaimukh subdivision of Churachandpur, which, along with four others (Henglep, Thanlon, Saikot, and Samulamlan), forms the epicentre of violence in Manipur. Claimed as 'liberated zones' by insurgents, safe hide-outs for as many as thirteen insurgent groups – each alleging that they represent a community or a hill tribal group or sub-group – are located here. Even non-tribal outfits from the Manipur valley claim to have a base in this district. Security forces, like the Assam Rifles, are also deployed in the area, and many of the insurgent groups that ostensibly come under the SoO (Suspension of Operation) agreement are to be found here too.

Despite the remote location and terrible roads – it takes two days to reach these villages by jeep from Lamka – there was no stopping HWA activists in their pursuit of justice. As the year wore on, intra-ethnic violence as well as clashes between State and non-State elements had reached such a point that villagers were fleeing to neighbouring Mizoram out of sheer helplessness. Many had horrifying stories to relate about the demands made by militant outfits at gunpoint. Pi J.L. Sawmi ("pi" is a prefix used locally as a mark of respect for an adult woman), the head of HWA and president of Churachandpur Joint Women's Union (CJWU), an umbrella body of various local women's groups, recalled in 2011, "During those days, the villagers would have to pay dearly if a demand or, rather, command – which extended to sexual favours – was not obeyed."

As HWA heightened its protest against the Tipaimukh rapes, moving from village to village, its activists came under all kinds of threats and their lives were in danger. Said Pi Sawmi, "We received innumerable unidentified calls, but ignored them or moved about incognito." The group also faced smear campaigns – the local media were very critical of their actions and alleged that they were engineering these protests at the behest of vested interests. But that, too, did not deter HWA. "We simply issued press releases and statements in response," said Pi Sawmi, coolly.

Within days, coordinated rallies and protests were held, both in Lamka and Delhi, which forced the Manipur government to set up the Rajkhowa Commission to look into the allegations. Ironically, although the crimes involved rape, the Commission did not include any health experts, let alone women investigators. The hearings and examinations of the victims were conducted in Parbung – the headquarters of Tipaimukh – with cross-examinations being undertaken by Human Rights Alert and the Manipur Forward Youth Front, both of which are valley-based, non-tribal bodies.

Apprehensive and demoralised by the turn of events, HWA leaders went knocking on the doors of the National Commission for Women (NCW) in Delhi in May 2006. "Fortunately, they heard us out patiently. Then-chairperson, Girija Vyas, and other members took the matter seriously," elaborated Pi Sawmi. Later, NCW member and Northeast-in-charge, Malini Bhattacharya, visited Tipaimukh and met the victims.

In her report, Bhattacharya stated that the girls who had undergone sexual assault and rape still suffered from headaches, listlessness and inability to concentrate, apart from various menstrual and urinary problems. Some reported impairment of eyesight and hearing, and there were also complaints of pain in the back and abdomen. Not surprisingly, every woman complained of living in fear. Bhattacharya also noted the abysmal lack of health care in the area: "There was neither hospital nor doctor, only a defunct primary health centre."

A major fear among the rape survivors was of having contracted HIV/AIDS as many of their attackers were known drug-pushers. There was also the stigma attached to being raped. In light of this, on NCW's recommendation, a free medical and trauma counselling camp was held in Parbung in November 2006. This move helped. According to Pi Sawmi, many of the victims felt better psychologically, as there was a lot of sharing with the full participation of HWA members. As one woman beneficiary said at that point, "When we talk about problems that only women can relate to, like abdominal pain, we feel better."

Several of the survivors left their homes to begin life anew in Mizoram or Meghalaya. But it has been difficult to erase the past completely. According to Pi Sawmi, these women – most working as domestic help – are still "living death", their hopes of marrying and settling down to a normal life completely extinguished.

The campaign also took a lot out of HWA activists. There was limited financial and legal support for their work. "All our funds were spent on travel and most of the time it was from our pocket. While NCW members were required to be ferried by helicopter, the HWA team would leave for Lamka two days ahead in order to be there on time," revealed Pi Sawmi.

Having lived through the conflict and seen its consequences at firsthand, the activists feel that a major gap in rehabilitation is the lack of support structures for women who undergo traumatic experiences. Given the local ignorance and illiteracy, the HWA team had a tough time dealing with the parents of rape survivors, most of whom wanted to keep the issue under wraps. It was only with time that they realised the importance of speaking out. The lack of health care infrastructure was another major challenge, with the survivors not knowing where to go or whom to approach for medical assistance.

But the biggest lesson learnt was the need for local women to organise and come together, especially in a district like Churachandpur where different communities and ethnic groups live cheek-by-jowl. That was why CJWU was convened in 2005. It comprises several community-based women organisations, including HWA, Zomi Mothers' Association, Kuki Women's Association, and Ima Leimaren Apunba Lup. The Union collectively resolved that any rape accused, no matter his ethnic background, should be awarded exemplary punishment.

Today, even as ethnic clashes continue to rage, CJWU has successfully intervened in several incidents. It is also exploring ways of keeping the original issue alive and is considering filing an RTI (Right to Information) petition regarding the action taken on the Rajkhowa Commission Report, which was submitted to the state government in 2007. So far, little appears to have come out of it.

Churachandpur's brave and feisty women activists want justice at all costs.

High Up in Assam's Hills, a Band of Peace-Builders

Ratna Bharali Talukdar

Karbi Anglong Hills District (Assam): The nightmare that Walson Teron, 51, went through in October 2003 has marked his life forever. His twelve-year-old daughter, Prativa, was gang-raped and Teron, who belongs to the Karbi tribe and lives in Langmili village in the Karbi Anglong Hills District of Assam, had to carry her on his back across a fourteen-kilometre-long hill route to the district headquarters of Diphu to get medical assistance. While he knew his child needed immediate medical care, the traumatised father was also wondering how he could file a report at the police station.

A day earlier, while Teron and his wife were out working

in the paddy fields near their home, their daughter had been gang-raped inside it by Assam police personnel. The police had been deployed there in an area domination exercise, as part of counter-insurgency operations against the Dima Halam Daoga (DHD), an insurgent outfit that was active in the districts of both Karbi Anglong and the adjacent North Cachar Hills.

For around a decade, the United Democratic People's Solidarity (UPDS), which represents the Karbi tribe, and DHD, which fights for the interests of the Dimasa tribe, have been engaged in an ethnic turf war. Hundreds of innocent tribals have been caught in the crossfire and in the ensuing counter-insurgency exercises.

As Teron made his way to Diphu with his daughter, he was advised to meet a group of women from the Karbi Nimso Chingthur Asong (KNCA), the apex women's body of the Karbi tribe, set up in 1986. When KNCA women learnt of the atrocity – one of the endless instances of abuse that women and children experience in this conflict-ridden area – they promptly decided to help. Experienced in fighting cases for female victims of conflict and ethnic violence, KNCA members also made immediate arrangements for Prativa's treatment at a district hospital.

They simultaneously spearheaded a movement to pressurise authorities to punish the guilty police personnel. This, however, was not an easy task. According to Kajektak Bipi, 45, the president of KNCA, senior officials in the district administration tried to conceal the evidence. However, the medical report made available by Teron established conclusively that rape had indeed been committed on the minor girl, following which KNCA registered a case at the Diphu Police Station. The organisation also moved the Assam State Commission for Women and the Assam Human Rights Commission in its campaign to seek justice for the child.

For Prativa, though, life was never the same again. KNCA's assistance could not spare her the social stigma that came with rape, and her poor, illiterate parents did not dare take her back home. Instead, the young victim found accommodation as domestic help in Diphu town, in the home of a Christian priest who was kind enough to ensure that the girl went to school. Hope resurfaced when Prativa was able to identify the culprits during an identification parade. KNCA members were constantly in touch with her and her parents during this entire period. The guilty police personnel were, thereafter, dismissed from service and sent to prison.

Meanwhile, even after Teron went back home in 2003 without his daughter, trauma and misfortune continued to plague him and his family. Two years after the assault on Prativa, he and all the residents of his village were forced to flee their homes when an ethnic clash between DHD and UPDS flared up on October 8, 2005, in different pockets of the district. The sudden attacks immediately claimed eleven lives. The extremists burnt down fifteen villages in the area. The attack and retaliation in the entire district resulted in the deaths of over 200 people and led to the displacement of about 49,000 people belonging to both tribes. The displaced persons had to take shelter in different relief camps. In 2006, they eventually settled down in Chachear Langso village, near Diphu town, having abandoned their original Langmili village.

The new settlers of Chachear Langso did not receive any rehabilitation assistance, and it was only in 2008 that the families were allotted houses under the Indira Awaas Yojna, a government social welfare scheme that provides housing for the rural poor in India. In addition, the families were allotted one acre of land each by the local Karbi people, so that they could return to agriculture. However, for jhum cultivation – the commonly practiced slash-and-burn technique used by tribal groups in the Northeast – they still had to go to conflict-prone Langmili.

Such have been the lived realities of the unfortunate inhabitants of Chachear Langso – and no one understands their difficulties better than KNCA members. Years of conflict have toughened its activists who are completely focused on their mission of helping and empowering the women and girls who are victims of the violence. Prativa's case is just one among the many they have taken up. In addition to such assistance, they stand by the affected families, just as they stood by Prativa's parents when they finally found the courage to bring their daughter back home in 2008.

Even as the organisation has continued to work towards its original goal of empowering Karbi women, it has also introduced some peace-building initiatives. Through its ninety-six branches and a joint action committee with the Dimasa Welfare Society – the women's body of the Dimasas – KNCA has undertaken peace-building programmes in the entire district, mobilising women to raise their voices for an end to this inter-tribal conflict.

Time and again, members hold peace rallies, visit relief camps of both tribes, distribute relief materials, and motivate the women to join in their initiatives. Said Bipi, in an interview in 2009, "The indiscriminate killing by militant outfits, the ethnic clashes, and the atrocities of security agencies on common people during search operations, have made our lives vulnerable. Many from traditional tribal families have become homeless, as they have had to abandon their original villages. From being farmers, most have become daily wage earners. Women and children are the worst sufferers of such migration and misery."

According to Mikon Rongpharpi, KNCA's vice president, even elderly women are sexually harassed by security agencies. In 2007, a fifty-five-year-old Karbi woman was raped by army jawans (soldiers) in Singhasan Timung village. As of mid-2009, her case was still pending in the Guwahati High Court. Owing to the extremely isolated location of the village and the age-related ailments of the victim, it was becoming difficult for her to appear in court on time and the possibility of justice ever being delivered was remote.

Bipi pointed out that even KNCA members are often subjected to harassment. For instance, on December 25, 2005, two Karbi girls, allegedly involved with the Karbi Longri North Cachar Hills Liberation Front (KLNLF), were apprehended by security personnel, and subsequently raped and killed. Later, the forces claimed that the bodies of the girls were not recovered. When KNCA, although it had nothing to do with the alleged involvement of the girls in militant activities, demanded that the details of the post-mortem report be disclosed, the police started harassing them and accusing them of having links with KLNLF.

Despite the challenges, there is good news in this story. KNCA's struggle for peace and more political power to the women of the region resulted in the election of the first Karbi woman, Kabon Ingtipi, to the Karbi Anglong Autonomous District Council. In 1996, Ingtipi was elected from the Hamren constituency as executive member.

This is how a small, determined group of women, far from the centres of power and overlooked by the rest of the country, has been making a significant difference to the lives of the forgotten people of these hills.

(*The names of the rape victim and her parents have been changed to protect their identities.*)

Hope among the Ruins: Fulara Wants to Farm Again

Ratna Bharali Talukdar

Goalpara (Assam): Meet Fulara Sira, 45, a tribal widow, mother of four, and the survivor of an ethnic clash that displaced her family for several months. As she made her way to the weekly prayer service at her local village church, Fulara did not forget to take along with her a small packet of rice. Despite the hunger and poverty this Garo tribeswoman from Ginogre village was experiencing herself, she always made it a point to donate her weekly share of rice, saved from family meals, to the church.

For the villagers of Ginogre in Goalpara district, located along the Assam-Meghalaya border, donating rice had become a routine. After community prayers every Sunday, the donated rice was collected and later sold to the needy at Rs 14 per kilogram instead of the market price of Rs 20-25. The money raised in this way was being put aside to fund the reconstruction of twenty-six homes and a church that had been burnt down during the January 2011 clashes between the Garo and Rabha tribes.

Ginogre was severely affected in that ethnic violence, which claimed at least twelve lives and instantly displaced 60,000 people from both the warring communities. Uprooted from their homes and hearths, the affected people were forced to take refuge in thirty-six relief camps set up in both Assam and Meghalaya.

Fortunately, due to the prompt action taken by both state administrations as well as assistance from local civil society organisations, the displaced villagers were able to go back home within six months. To restart life, each family was given a grant of Rs 10,000 and three bundles of galvanised corrugated iron sheets to construct their home.

Surely this had to be one of those rare stories of success where the internally displaced were concerned. But the reality on the ground was very different. Merely returning the victims to their destroyed villages could not make for a happy beginning. Where was the infrastructure to live a normal life – a school, a health centre; where were the livelihood opportunities that could enable families to earn money and put food on the table?

Though the problems were many, it was the lack of employment that was turning out be the biggest spoiler. The ethnic clashes had destroyed the age-old economic interdependence between the Garos and the Rabhas, vital for the sustenance of both communities – and the local authorities were completely indifferent to this. Moreover, being illiterate and extremely poor, the people did not know how to access even those government schemes and benefits that were meant exclusively for tribals.

Ginogre village, in fact, was the perfect example of institutional neglect. Take healthcare. While the state

Department of Health was supposed to appoint Accredited Social Health Activists, or volunteer health workers, for every village – and these women have indeed successfully intervened elsewhere – there were none in Ginogre, located in one of the most malaria-prone areas of the country.

In fact, the nearest health centre was located in Mendipathar, some four kilometres away, and the road that led to the skeletal facility was so bad that most women opted to have their deliveries at home. Water-borne diseases were the other major health concern. Families were dependent on dug wells for drinking water, which was often contaminated with sewage. In terms of basic nutrition, the rice meant for Below Poverty Line people was distributed only once every two months, and card-holders got only ten kilos instead of the government-sanctioned monthly quota of thirty-five kilos.

Another government scheme that eluded the community was the disbursement of pensions. Fulara had suffered on that count too. Though her husband, Darshan Marak, a primary school teacher, had died of an unidentified disease in 2008, she had not been able to secure his pension even three years after his demise.

Before the clashes ruined her life, Fulara was making ends meet by living off her small plot of agricultural land. Along with a rubber plantation of nearly a hectare, she was able to feed her family for four months of the year through farming and somehow managed to keep things going for the rest of the time. But, in the fighting that broke out, everything got burnt down, including her livestock and home. The family fled to the East Garo Hills of Meghalaya, close to the Assam border, the traditional home of their tribespeople, and then languished in makeshift relief camps for over three months.

Although she came back to Ginogre, survival was challenging. "For some days we had to beg for survival. Though this is against our norms and customs, there was nothing else we could do. Now, my elder son, who is a student of Class XII, works as a daily wage earner to feed us," Fulara revealed when we met her in 2011.

Fulara's was not the only family in the village that was struggling with its circumstances. The violence had resulted in widespread penury. Yet, hope came to them in the shape of a unique economic initiative. The Assam branch of the Indian Red Cross Society (IRCS) and the International Committee of the Red Cross had joined forces to start the Micro Economic Initiative Programme (MEIP), aimed at improving the living conditions of the "most affected" families.

Elaborated Laba Kumar Sharma, who headed the field activities of MEIP's pilot project, "The MEIP aimed at providing actual rehabilitation to conflict victims by making available productive material to them on the basis of their traditional livelihood and needs. It followed a very distinctive procedure to identify the most affected families instead of just distributing something in the name of rehabilitation."

To achieve this, the programme laid emphasis on phased activities, which included a profile assessment of the affected villages in order to identify the most affected people; a house-to-house survey in these identified villages to find out more about the traditional skills on which these families had relied prior to the conflict situation. This was followed by identifying the actual needs of the most affected, in coordination with the local administrative authorities, and then distributing materials after consultation with the village headman and other concerned persons. Measures were also laid down to monitor and evaluate the efficacy of the intervention.

MEIP started off by reaching out to four of the most affected villages, which covered both the affected ethnic groups: Ginogre and Puthimari in Goalpara district of Assam and Genang and Thapa Dangre of the East Garo Hills District of Meghalaya. Said Deba Prasad Sarma, planning and reporting coordinator, IRCS, Assam, "We distributed productive materials in accordance with the previous sources of livelihood of the affected people, and since such materials are ready-to-use, the beneficiaries can resume their economic activity from the very next day itself."

In order to monitor the use of the assistance provided

through MEIP and to assess the economic worthiness of the income generating activities, all the families were asked to open a bank account in a financial institution near them before they were given the productive grant. They were also instructed to deposit a certain amount of money earned through their work in that account.

Significantly, MEIP had already been successfully implemented for conflict victims of Darrang-Udalguri districts, which had also seen an outbreak of ethnic violence between the religious minority community and the Bodos in 2008. Over 1,00,000 people had been displaced in those incidents.

In 2011, Fulara was full of new energy. A beneficiary of MEIP, she was completely focused on reviving her small farm and rubber plantation. She had even got Red Cross survey volunteers to visit the site where her luscious trees had once stood and she had identified the places where she wanted to plant them once again. She was all geared up to start earning an independent livelihood. This was the only way, she believed, to forget the bitterness of the immediate past and move on to a hopefully happier future.

Women of Nandigram Come Together in Conflict

Aditi Bhaduri

Nandigram (West Bengal): In March 2007, and then again in November that year, the streets of Kolkata, the state capital of West Bengal, were overflowing with people who expressed their outrage over the political violence that was unleashed on the hapless inhabitants of Nandigram.

This rural pocket in the district of East Midnapore – now renamed Purba Medinipur – had turned into a battleground with the then-ruling party of the state, the Communist Party of India (Marxist) [CPI(M)], pitted against the Trinamool Congress-backed Bhoomi Ucched Pratirodh Committee

(BUPC), over the conversion of fertile agricultural land into a Special Economic Zone (SEZ).

How did the Nandigram face-off unfold? In December 2006, the CPI(M) government issued a notice of land acquisition to set up an SEZ. Violent protests by BUPC followed. As the situation began to spin out of control, the notification was withdrawn, but the violence continued for another eleven months. It was only after the industries agreed to move out of the region permanently that things begin to simmer down.

Two years later, in 2009, the people of Nandigram were still trying to pick up the pieces of their shattered lives. Among them, it was the women who had emerged as the face of hope thanks to the activities of the Matangini Mahila Samiti (MMS) – the Matangini women's committee. Set up during the conflict in July 2007, the organisation had been providing moral, legal, and social support to the women of Nandigram ever since.

MMS – which draws its name from Matangini Hazra, a martyr from Nandigram, who heroically led a procession against the British during the 1942 Quit India Movement – was started by local women like Radharani Ari, Krishna Mondol, and Chabi Maity, with help from Kolkata-based activists, Deblina Chakaborty and Juita Das. Many of the local women who joined MMS had themselves experienced assault, molestation or rape during the Nandigram clashes. They were attacked precisely because they were at the frontlines of the battle from the very first uprising against the SEZ that took place on January 3, 2007.

Radharani explained why local women felt so strongly about the issue: "We worked on the land too. If it had been taken away for monetary compensation, the money would have gone to the men. Even the jobs would have been for the men. What would have happened to us? We would have had to beg from the men in our families to survive."

The MMS, which came into being after the first round of violence, initially set out to educate women about the concept of the SEZ, so that they were aware of the forces they were up against and the strategies they would need. The sessions were conducted once a month by the Kolkata activists. Most MMS members acknowledged that it was these initial meetings that were responsible for the confidence with which Nandigram's women fought for their rights. Not only did they become aware of land rights, women's rights and violations committed by the authorities, they were also able to raise their voices against various social malpractices with considerable success. Later, they managed to keep a close watch on the elected representatives of the area and even continued their work on issues like health and education for girls and women – issues that desperately needed to be addressed in Nandigram much after the violence subsided.

Habiba Bibi was one of MMS's transformed women of MMS. Hailing from Garchakreberia, a predominantly Muslim village, where for years women had been told that Islam forbade them from becoming socially and politically active, Habiba became an agent of change once she joined MMS. She soon realised that this was just another ploy by a patriarchal society to control women. So she spoke with local women to try to make them see things her way. She argued that God wanted people to speak up against evil, and since the forced acquisition of land was not ethical, women could organise and protest without fear. Habiba's argument was convincing, and many Muslim women came out of their homes to participate in MMS meetings.

In July 2007, came another breakthrough when MMS members were successful in shutting down five liquor shops in the villages of Shonachura, Gokulnagar, and Garchakraberia. Recalled Krishna Mondol, "We realised that alcohol had a terrible impact on our men and it caused a lot of problems for the family. Men who drink often beat up their wives and also squandered all the household money on alcohol."

In November 2007, when the harmads – as CPI(M) political activists are known locally – launched an assault against the people, the police simply stood by without intervening. It was only when MMS women threatened to confiscate their weapons that the police stepped in to take control.

However, some successes apart, MMS women soon found out that transforming attitudes was actually a long, arduous battle. Time and again, they faced opposition from their own families. Deblina Chakroborty, the activist associated with MMS, recalled the time the husband of a member barged in on a monthly gathering because his wife had not served him lunch before coming there. However, when he saw the number of women gathered, he quietly went back home. Krishna Mondol had a hilarious episode to relate as well. Once, her husband actually hid her sari so that she would not be able to go out of the house for a meeting. But she was adamant and he relented on the condition that she let him accompany her. Krishna instantly agreed. Eventually, even her husband became an enthusiastic MMS activist!

In any conflict, women are the soft targets, and the maelstrom in Nandigram was no exception. Not surprisingly then, all of MMS's work is focused on helping women caught in the crossfire to reclaim their lost dignity. In 2007, the High Court of Kolkata ordered the state government to give a compensation of Rs 200,000 to victims of rape and sexual assault, though the administration managed to get a stay on that order. But there are women like Radharani, who are determined to fight this. This grandmother created waves when she claimed that the harmads had raped her. "It was not easy for me, but I came forward because I had nothing to lose," she said. What helped her take the decision to speak out was the knowledge that she wasn't alone in her struggle. "All my village sisters are with me and MMS continues to give me enormous moral support. They have provided us with a new perspective: they've shown us that women are not helpless instruments to be used by men," she said.

Lakhi Rani Das was another victim of the violence. Both her husband, Pritish, and her mother-in-law were badly beaten up during the conflict. The burden of keeping the family going entirely fell on Lakhi, who earned some money by helping out in her neighbour's tea stall. It is for women like her that MMS has proved to be a great source of strength, besides providing a window to a wider world.

Delivering Health Care at Gunpoint in Salboni

Ajitha Menon

Paschim Medinipur (West Bengal): Sombari Hemrom gave birth to a premature baby boy in June 2010 in Kalaimuri village that comes under Salboni block in the Maoist-affected district of West Midnapore – now named Paschim Medinipur – in West Bengal. "I thought I would die, my baby would die," recalled the twenty-eight-year-old woman.

Fortunately, Sombari's worst fears did not come true. Timely intervention from the doctor and nurse at a makeshift health centre in the village saved both their lives. It's another matter that the said health centre's 'doctor' was a quack, and the 'nurse' an untrained attendant.

How did this alternative health delivery system come about? Explained Aarti Mahato, 55, of Kalaimuri village: "The insurgency started in this region around 2007-08 and reached its peak in 2009-10. Government officials, including the health department staff posted here, fled the area fearing for their lives. There was no one left to run the government offices, schools or health centres."

Incidentally, it was this lack of development and basic amenities in Paschim Medinipur, one of the most backward regions of the eastern state, that has often been cited as the primary reason for the local people's support of the Maoist insurgency. For example, according to 2007 figures posted by the district administration, Salboni block had a population of about 1,65,000. For these rural residents, the state government provided just one hospital and three Primary Health Centres (PHCs). Apart from these, there was one central government health undertaking and one privately-run nursing home. The total number of beds in the block stood at seventy-nine, while there were only twelve doctors on the rolls. This, in a region where malnutrition was high, where skin diseases like scabies were common, where tuberculosis and malaria were rife, and where diarrhoea-related illnesses were flourishing due to substandard drinking water, bad hygiene, and a poor diet.

Even the few doctors and nurses on the rolls hardly made an appearance at the PHCs or the health sub-centres. According to Pradyut Mahato, who was at one point a member of the Maoist-backed People's Committee Against Police Atrocities (PCAPA), there were times when only a compounder could be seen selling medicines which were actually meant for free distribution. He stoutly maintained that it was wrong to say that the Maoist movement had destroyed health facilities in the district – they were negligible in any case. One of the reasons why PCAPA received local support at the height of the insurgency was because it had started its own health centres to help the rural people. Said Mahato, "We used the village women to run these centres."

That was where the unqualified 'doctors' and untrained 'nurses' came into being. In fact, Aarti was one of them. She explained how she became a nurse: "The situation was terrible. Many of our men and women joined the movement voluntarily while others were forced to do so at gunpoint. In any case, there was no work to be found. Our children could not go to school and there was hardly any food in the house. But worst of all, there was no one to care for pregnant women, deliver babies or even treat a snake bite. So I agreed to be a health attendant when the PCAPA asked me." She, along with two other women, took up nursing duties in the village.

PCAPA set up about twenty-five to thirty such medical centres during 2009-10 in different villages in blocks like Salboni and Binpur-I, where the violence-affected village of Lalgarh is located. Local doctors and nursing attendants either served in these camps voluntarily or were forced to do so at gunpoint. Several untrained people were also asked to chip in. Each of these centres catered to about 100-150 patients on a daily basis.

Jyotsna Tudu, 25, a trained nurse serving in Lalgarh, recalled that difficult time: "Money was at a premium. People had no food to eat. Ration shops were closed and there was no agricultural produce. The Maoists extorted Rs 10-20 and a kilo of rice from every household that could afford it. Families were often left with nothing. Malnutrition became one of the primary health concerns in the region."

It was in such conditions that PCAPA arranged for free medicines and also distributed glucose and Electral powder gratis. But there were too many people suffering and very little relief. According to Dr. R. Dey, former block medical officer of Chandra block in Paschim Medinipur, the government tried its best to reach medical facilities to the remotest areas in the district, but the threat from the Maoists was just too great for the medical staff to handle. In fact, Dr. Dey claimed that the health centres set up by PCAPA were nothing but a front for Maoist operations.

According to Tarulata Mahato, 38, who acted as a compounder at a PCAPA-supported health centre in Binpur-I block, when the joint paramilitary operations against the Maoists began in July 2009, the first targets were these health centres. "The forces claimed that Maoists were being given shelter and treated there. But how were we to differentiate between a common villager and a Maoist when someone came in with high fever, bouts of vomiting or a snake bite?" she asked.

By agreeing to work at these PCAPA-run medical centres, the poor villagers were only looking to help each other out in times of adversity, but even that effort had to be carried out under life-threatening conditions. Said Kalpana Mahato, 45, of Bhulabera village, "I am a trained nursing attendant. I used to work at the government-run PHC before the officials ran away. So, when the PCAPA ordered me to work in their health centre, I agreed so that at least the people could avail of some medical care. Moreover, if I had refused, the Maoists would have shot me."

When the paramilitary forces started gaining ground in the insurgency-affected district, PCAPA-run medical centres were closed down. But it took a while for the government PHCs to begin functioning again and this gap in terms of health services caused untold suffering to a population that was in dire need of medical attention. Srimati Mahato, 60, of Binpur-I, for instance, found herself in a difficult situation at that point: "My daughter-in-law was six months pregnant. There was no staff at the nearest health centre, which was anyway twenty-five kilometres away. She had not seen a doctor for months and I was frantic with worry about her safety and the life of her unborn child."

Instances like this explained why local people had come to accept the alternative health delivery system set up by the PCAPA, despite its shotgun methods and subversive agenda. As Mahato argued, "If the state government ignores the needs of the people, they will have to do something about it. We realised the need of the people and that's why we ran these medical camps ourselves."

Clearly, if there is one lesson to be learnt from Salboni it is this: if the State ignores health care, it creates grounds for alienation and conflict.

Scars of War: Kargil's Blowback in Kangra

Nirupama Dutt

Kangra (Himachal Pradesh): Over a decade after the war that claimed their young sons and husbands had ended, a sense of loss was still very much a part of the lives of mothers and wives in the Kangra district of Himachal Pradesh (HP). This is a region from where many young men have traditionally served in the army – a tradition that dates back to pre-Mughal times. The two-month war, which broke out after Pakistani soldiers and militants infiltrated the Indian side of the Line of Control, started in late May 1999 in the Kargil district of Jammu & Kashmir.

The impact of the war can be felt to this day in the tea garden town of Palampur in HP. Two promising young officers,

Lieutenant Saurabh Kalia and Captain Vikram Batra, came from this town and their close relatives continue to grieve for them.

For Vijay Kalia, a former Sanskrit teacher in her mid-fifties, things have never been the same since the badly mutilated body of her twenty-two-year-old son, Saurabh, was delivered at her doorstep in June 1999. When we met her in 2009, the grief-stricken woman said that she had not even caught a glimpse of her son in his uniform – "He was martyred even before his first paycheque arrived."

It was Saurabh's dream to join the Indian army even while he was studying at the Kendriya Vidyalya (central government school) at Palampur. This, despite the fact that his father, N.K. Kalia, was a senior scientist. Commissioned from the Indian Military Academy, Dehradun, Lt. Kalia was posted with the 4 Jat Regiment (Infantry) to serve in the Kargil sector and was one of the first officers to be killed in that war. He was captured along with five other soldiers at Bajrang Post and was brutally tortured for three weeks before being shot dead.

The hall on the first floor of the Kalia residence has been converted into a museum to Saurabh's memory. Here, the young officer's uniforms, unused toiletries, and photographs have been preserved with care. Vijay and her husband spend a lot of time in this room when they are at home. Said Saurabh's father, "Whatever monetary compensation we got, we donated to charity. If the government wanted to help us, they should have taken up the issue of ensuring that every captured soldier is accorded dignified treatment on both sides of the border. Sometimes I wish his mother had not seen his mutilated body." Of course, Vijay was quick to add, "Everyone has to die one day. It gives me satisfaction that our Saurabh laid his life down for the country."

Similar sentiments were voiced by the parents of Param Veer Chakra Capt. Vikram Batra of the 13 Jammu & Kashmir Rifles. The young captain, fond of driving and country music, shared his birth month with the famed patriot-revolutionary

Bhagat Singh, and like his icon, he too wanted to make his mark on the country's history.

Sorrow seemed to have found a permanent dwelling place in the eyes of Kamal Kant Batra, as she remembered how her son had rejected a job with the merchant navy for a career in the army. "He told me that a career in the merchant navy would mean good money but he wanted to do something more than just make money. For us, his death is, of course, an irretrievable loss, but he did us and the whole nation proud," she said. Meanwhile, the Batras, who worked at the Kendriya Vidyalya in Palampur, are providing support to others who have suffered experiences similar to theirs.

In fact, both the Kalias and the Batras are active in army welfare societies as well as social and educational institutions. They enjoy a lot of respect in Kangra and have become opinion shapers, sometimes even being called upon to counsel others.

According to Kishwar Ahmed Shirali, a psychologist and women's activist based in Sidhbarhi, some thirty kilometres from Palampur, "Glorifying patriotism and celebrating the bravery of young soldiers who become cannon fodder is a way of coping with loss. It is very difficult to lose a child and society tries to compensate for this loss by according honour to the close relatives of those who are killed in battle. Every other village in this region has a gate dedicated to one young martyr or another. But actually each of these deaths is in itself a strong appeal against war and conflict."

If there are inconsolable parents, there are grief-stricken wives as well. There are cases where soldiers have died leaving behind teenaged brides with whom they had lived for barely a month. For these young women, losing their husband was not the only blow. They have also had to deal with relatives trying to lay their hands on the monetary compensation due to them. Take the case of Sudarshana Devi of Jiya village in Kangra. She was just twenty when her husband, rifleman Rakesh Chand of the J&K Rifles, serving in Kargil, died on June 14, 1999. During his last rites, she pushed aside the village elders and offered a shoulder to his coffin as it was being taken for cremation.

But after the tragedy, came the travails. Her husband's family called her a witch who had killed their son. A bitter battle ensued for the compensation that was made in Rakesh's name when Sudarshana decided to remarry, after being encouraged to do so by people like Vijay Kalia. Eventually, Rakesh's pension was divided between his mother and his wife. With the money she received, Sudarshana built a house and married Jagdish Raj, a cab driver. Today, she is a mother of two children, and the couple runs a petrol pump at Tahliwal in Una district.

While Sudarshana has managed to rebuild her life, it has certainly not been an easy process. "Apart from the few people who know me, I am judged poorly for having remarried. My marriage has remained a subject of gossip even after all these years. I still cherish the memory of Rakesh and can never forget him, but life has to go on," she said.

There are also instances where widows have been married off to their younger brothers-in-law – a very old practice in this region – so that the compensation they received would remain within the family. Sometimes such arrangements were made after forcing the widow to fall in line, but other women have actively opted to remain within the families of their deceased husbands. Take Smridhi Kanta of Jahu village in Bilaspur district. Smridhi married her childhood sweetheart, rifleman Deep Chand, in February 1999, widowed that June, and delivered a baby girl in December. Her husband's parents offered to marry her to their other son, Vijay, also a rifleman with the J&K Rifles, who returned home after seven years of service. Smridhi thought over it and then agreed. "The wife of Deep's commanding officer advised me to go ahead. Life moves on, but I always draw strength from the love I got from Deep. Our daughter is cherished by the whole family because she is Deep's living memory," she said.

The Kargil war guns have fallen silent. But the Indo-Pak border is not free of conflict. Bodies of dead soldiers continue to be brought home every now and then. Monica Devi of Tang village in Yole Cantonment, Kangra district, was six months pregnant in 2006 when the remains of her husband, Ravi Kumar, were repatriated from the Poonch sector in Kashmir. With her young daughter, Prakriti, she lives in her late husband's home. Pointing to photographs in her wedding album, she said, "Life has given me a cruel shock. I now live only for this child."

Said her aunt, Mishro Devi, who organises mahila mandals (women's groups) in Kangra, "It's only after four or more years of such a death that a family can take the decision to marry the widow to her younger brother-in-law, otherwise the wounds are still raw." She added that she had counselled her sister and brother-in-law to be kind to their unfortunate daughter-in-law who was not yet twenty-five-years-old at that time.

Explained Mishro Devi, "Families here have small landholdings but it is rocky land. So joining the army is a way of making a career and providing for the future. Unfortunately, such a career also includes the danger of a premature date with death and misery for those left behind."

Health Care Workers Deliver Hope in Maoist Country

Sarada Lahangir

Koraput (Odisha): The eastern state of Odisha has the fourth highest number of fatalities due to conflict among Indian states, after West Bengal, Chhattisgarh, and Jharkhand. Within Odisha, it is Koraput district that has witnessed the highest number of such deaths. In 2010, there were at least forty-three such fatalities.

In such a situation, imagine the plight of poverty-stricken

communities living in the hinterland when it comes to accessing health care. People here are sometimes unable to get treatment even for those who are grievously ill, either because health personnel refuse to come fearing attack, or because there is no source of transportation due to an outbreak of violence or a strike call.

In these extremely disturbed conditions, where there is no doctor and where there is constant fear caused by the endless cycle of Maoist violence and state reprisal, it is the Accredited Social Health Activist (ASHA) who has lived up to her name, asha, which in Hindi means hope.

Nobel Laureate Amartya Sen once observed that ASHAs are the "God of many hopes and the beast of all burdens". Many in Koraput would vouch for the truth of those words, and among them would be Barti Jani, 23, of Mademgandi village in Potangi block. It is because of the ASHA of her village, Moti Jani, that Barti is alive today. "I owe my life to Moti didi (elder sister)," said the young woman. It was Moti who had her taken to a hospital at two o'clock on a stormy night in 2010.

Recalled Barti, "I was three months pregnant and suddenly experienced a severe pain in my lower abdomen. The hospital at Potangi is about seven kilometres from our village. My husband asked the neighbours to help, but nobody came forward because people don't leave their homes at night fearing Maoist attacks. At that point, Moti didi – who lives in another hamlet two kilometres away – arrived. She convinced a villager to lend us his rickshaw. With my husband pulling it, we could reach the hospital at around 4:30 a.m. I was admitted and operated upon immediately."

Dr. N.K. Kar of Potangi hospital, too, was all praise for Moti: "Barti had an ectopic pregnancy. The tube had ruptured and she was bleeding internally. If she hadn't been brought on time, we couldn't have saved her. The whole credit for that one life being saved must go to ASHA Moti Jani, who showed immense courage in bringing her to hospital at night, when people are too scared to travel on these roads even during the day."

In nearby Phulpadar village, a young man, Sarbeswar Muduli, is also full of gratitude. Phulpadar, around eighteen kilometres from the headquarters of Koraput district, is one of its most inaccessible pockets. To reach here, one would have to hire a vehicle for the first fifteen kilometres and then cover the rest of the distance of three kilometres on foot. Three years ago, Sarbeswar lost his wife during childbirth because they could not make it to the hospital in time. When he remarried, he made sure his new wife's pregnancy was supervised by "ASHA didi, Minati Gauda". It was she who took the couple to the Koraput district hospital where the expectant mother had a safe delivery.

There are stories like these everywhere in this tribal district. Talk to the ASHAs themselves, and their commitment to their work comes through. Sabitri Bisoyee, 35, became an ASHA some four years ago. She covers thirteen villages, a territory of twelve to fifteen square kilometres of forested terrain. And she does this on foot. Said Sabitri, "Most of the time, there is no transportation available and the ongoing conflict between the state and extremists has only made things worse."

Although the government had promised cycles and mobile phones to women like her, so far nothing has reached them. Most ASHAs come from poor families and are in dire need of a regular income themselves. Parvati Dora, 32, who has studied up to Class VI, described her situation: "I belong to a very poor family and it is difficult for us to live on my elderly father's wages. It was to help the family out that I became an ASHA. We got trained to do many things, like collecting blood samples, distributing medicines, and providing general primary health care."

Even as the fear factor looms large, ASHAs try to remain focused on saving the patient's life. But this is often difficult given the poor facilities in primary health centres and the general absence of doctors. Many have reported that they feel "helpless" in the face of such challenges. Women like Parvati have, in fact, largely shouldered the responsibility of delivering health care in rural Odisha, and Dr. R.N. Das, the chief district medical officer of Koraput, had no hesitation in agreeing with this observation: "It is difficult to get trained doctors, and at least 30-40 per cent of government medical posts lie vacant because no one wants to come here to work. We ultimately we have to rely on these poor women," he said.

A senior consultant and ASHA coordinator for the National Rural Health Mission, Sushant Nayak, who is based in state capital Bhubaneswar, has estimated that in Odisha, as of 2011, there were more than 40,000 ASHAs in place, with Koraput alone accounting for 1,400 such women.

Despite their undoubted importance, the issue of fair compensation for ASHAs hardly figures in public discussions. About 70 per cent of the total income of ASHAs is earned through the Janani Suraksha Yojana (Safe Motherhood Scheme), under which they are required to bring pregnant women to health institutions for their deliveries. They receive Rs 600 per delivery, including Rs 250 for transportation. However, they get nothing for their work in antenatal and postnatal care.

In fact, according to a report of the Orissa Technical and Management Support Team (TMST), the ASHAs of the under-serviced, relatively inaccessible Koraput-Bolangir-Kalahandi region are paid 25 per cent less than those elsewhere in the state. According to TMST calculations, as of 2011, the potential monthly income of an ASHA here was Rs 1,800. However, on an average, she earned Rs 954, and often actually received only Rs 721. "Payments to ASHAs are incentive-based, but sometimes we can't even get the Rs 100 we are supposed to be paid as incentive per delivery. In all, I earn about Rs 700-800 a month," said Sabitri, who has to help support a family of six.

Bhanumati Gadaba, an ASHA of Maliguda village in the district, explained the lags: "We are often paid in bulk for several months of work. There are no written statements for payments made, which means we are unable to verify whether the amount we get is correct. There is also no system to reimburse us if there are errors." A common complaint among these women has been that they lack job security since they don't officially exist on any employment rolls. In fact, as Sabitri pointed out, even ASHAs with a decade of experience are yet to be regularised.

C.H. Shantakar, a local social activist, has argued that more should be done for these women: "Additional incentives should be made available to them so that they can play their designated role as community mobilisers and service providers. They also need skill enhancement so that they can conduct themselves with greater confidence."

Seeing Koraput's ASHAs in action brings Amartya Sen's observation back to mind. These unsung women do indeed play the role of God by saving lives. But they certainly need to be given the recognition they deserve and a just monetary compensation for their efforts.

Kandhamal's Wonder Women Fight Hate

Eliza Parija

Kandhamal (Odisha): It was Laxmi Priya Parida's moment of truth. One morning in 2008, this woman from Bramunigaon village located in Odisha's Kandhamal district, answered a knock on the door only to be confronted by a group of men holding swords behind their backs.

"They started threatening me. They asked me why, despite being the daughter of a Hindu, I was not 'participating' in the attack against Christians," recalled Laxmi, who is in her mid-thirties. They also accused her and her family of supporting Christians and said that they would impose a fine of Rs 20,000 on the family for this 'offence'. The intruders did not stop at that; they also issued a threat to kill Laxmi and burn down her home if the family did not fall in line.

Kandhamal district was convulsed by attacks on the local Christian tribal community in late 2007, after the murder of Vishwa Hindu Parishad leader, Swami Lakshmananda Saraswati, who had been working against Christian conversions of tribals in the region. The assassination was allegedly committed by Maoist insurgents in the area, but it was the tribal Christian community that was held responsible, and it came to be the focus of murderous assaults which led to the destruction of numerous homes, houses of worship, and educational institutions in the area. Some 50,000 people were estimated to have been displaced in several waves of violence that raged in the area, well into 2008.

Laxmi, a social worker by profession, had been working to rehabilitate those who had fled in terror in the wake of the attacks and also encourage people from all communities to maintain peace in her village. That morning, she did not lose her nerve while confronting the mob at the door. She explained to the agitators that on no account would her family take part in any attacks on local Christians. She also appealed to the men to stop spreading more violence. "I knew I was pleading with a group of people who had lost all sense of humanity and rationality. Inside of me, I was scared. I also knew that my family was terrorised by the recent events, but my conscience wouldn't allow me to bow before a misdirected mob," she said, when we spoke to her in 2009. What helped her muster up her courage was the memory of the frightened faces of all those people who had fled to nearby forests when the violence had broken out and who were forced to go without food and water for days.

Married to a Christian, Laxmi found that this fact sometimes worked in her favour. "When I approach ordinary people from both the Hindu and Christian communities, they welcome me. But then there are times when the fundamentalists consider me a traitor," she said. The activist worked for an Odisha-based organisation, the Council of Professional Social Workers, that focuses on securing livelihoods for tribals, Dalits, and the rural poor. Ever since the ethno-religious conflict broke out in the region, Laxmi, along with her colleagues, started focusing on recovery and peace-building through Self-Help Groups (SHGs) covering eight panchayats in the district. Explained Laxmi, "We knew that some people in our village – with a population of nearly 8,000 – had been given arms, which if used could have led to a volatile situation. However, we were successful in convincing members of both communities to abjure any show of hatred and violence, at least in our village."

Like Laxmi, several women in Kandhamal made efforts to spread the message of peace and harmony between the different communities. Ratnamala Kanhara, 20, from Pubingia village, was one of them. Although very young, she had been personally affected by the riots and had vowed to bring people together. During an early explosion of violence, her father had been murdered by fundamentalists for protesting the killing of a person, and her family had been forced to flee to the forests fearing further attacks. But Ratnamala maintained that she did not harbour any animosity towards any religion even though her father had been murdered in the name of religion. "My mother, two sisters and I want to make people aware that killing in the name of religion is abhorrent," she said.

Ratnamala had spoken out about her experiences while participating in a training camp on peace organised by a coalition of NGOs in Kandhamal in December 2008. She was one of the nearly 150 young girls who had participated in a peace-building measure at the Tumudibandha and G. Udaygiri blocks in the district at that point.

Despite such initiatives involving women of all ages and regardless of the heartening stories of individual courage like that of Laxmi, the participation of women in peace-building measures in Kandhamal had remained confined largely to the informal level. The team of Women's International League for Peace and Freedom and Women in Security, Conflict Mitigation and Peace, which visited the district in January 2009, had observed in its report that women were given low priority in conflict resolution. It noted that although the UN Security Council Resolution 1325 stresses "the important role of women in the prevention and resolution of conflicts and in peace-building" and the need to increase women's "role in decision-making with regard to conflict prevention and resolution", there were no women on the peace committees in Kandhamal.

This, despite the fact that several women were victims of violence precisely because of their public positions. The rape of a Catholic nun at K. Nuagaon in August 2008 was a case in point. Ludhia Diggal, an anganwadi worker from Tikabali village, narrated another incident of a woman health worker who was murdered and her body mutilated. "Several women have been victims of violence during the riots, but their suffering has hardly been reported," she said.

Commented Vasanth Kannabiran of the Hyderabad-based women's resource centre, Asmita, "Women peace-keepers are not at the negotiating and decision-making table and remain confined to the level of overseeing relief camps. It should be remembered that building peace is not just welfare work, it is about educating people, changing mindsets and protesting violence whenever it occurs."

In response, state government sources argued that its peace-keeping efforts focus on the entire community and not just women. They also pointed out that the government has always supported the participation of women's SHGs and women's organisations in these interventions.

Experts, however, emphasise that the significance of women's involvement in peace-keeping is not just because of the specific problems they face as a result of the conflict, but because they are uniquely placed to educate their communities on the values of social harmony. Observed Professor Asha Hans, former head of the School of Women's Studies, Utkal University, Odisha, "Rather than integrating women in the peace-building process, they are often used as pawns in conflict situations, as was illustrated in Kandhamal."

There have been instances of hundreds of women in

Kandhamal defying the ban on five or more people gathering at a particular spot, which was enforced during the riots. They demonstrated before police stations and government offices demanding the release of those arrested on charges of rioting. But the problem that emerged time and again in these mobilisations was the lack of unity. They remained divided along religious and political fault lines.

The Independent Tribunal on Kandhamal Violence of 2008, consisting of eminent jurists and activists, had noted that there was tremendous potential for peace-building in Khandamal. Its report pointed out that in 1994, for instance, during the riots between Dalit Christians and tribal adivasis, mainly as a result of conflict over economic resources like land, women from different tribes and groups had played a leadership role in bringing about social harmony.

Such historical precedents must not be forgotten. Khandamal demonstrated how vital the role of women is in post-conflict scenarios.

After the Delhi Riots, How Women Rebuilt their Lives

Nirupama Dutt

Mohali (Punjab): A large oil painting of a tall and handsome Sikh dominates Lakhbir Kaur's modest sitting room in Kumbra village in Mohali, near Chandigarh. She explained how it came about: "I found a small black-and-white picture of my father in a relative's album and my husband got a friend of his to make this painting for us."

For Lakhbir, the painting is a constant reminder of the days that followed the assassination of India's first woman prime minister, Indira Gandhi, on October 31, 1984, when Delhi came to be engulfed in a horrific anti-Sikh pogrom that saw the killing of 2,733 Sikhs in the capital alone, according to official figures. "We were sitting in our home in Delhi's Sultanpuri watching television when a mob gathered in the neighbourhood and started to go on the rampage. Our Muslim neighbours immediately gave us shelter and advised my father to cut his hair and beard," recalled Lakhbir.

Deedar Singh, Lakhbir's father, dismissed the idea. After retiring from the army, he had been working as a security guard in a private company. And since he was also the president of the local Congress party office in Sultanpuri, he believed he was safe. "Both my brothers were out and he went to look for them. He asked us to stay with the neighbours and said he would return shortly. We never saw him again, not even his remains," said Lakhbir.

Lakhbir's mother was one of seven sisters, six of whom lived in different parts of the city. Several of her cousins were killed in that riot. After moving to their neighbour's home, the family members who had survived moved to a camp in Delhi, and from there to a gurudwara in Mohali, Punjab. Lakhbir was only sixteen years old then. It was decided by the larger family that since it was difficult for a young, fatherless girl to survive without protection, Lakhbir's marriage should be arranged. And so it was. Her first child, a daughter, was born a year later. She never went back to her Delhi home. There was nothing to go back to – everything had been burnt down.

Even today, this mother of two daughters and a son breaks down while talking about that violent time in her life. "The scars will always remain, but with the support of my husband we have nurtured a sense of love rather than hate in our children," she said with satisfaction.

Sharing similar stories of terror and loss are Kashmir Kaur and Ravindar Kaur, who fled the capital during the riots and sought security in Punjab. They too have rebuilt their broken lives in a spirit of camaraderie and affection and are making significant contributions to their immediate society in different ways. After the great disruption in their lives, these riot-affected women did whatever they could in order to survive: from tailoring clothes to making pickles, from setting up small shops to doing voluntary work in gurudwaras. Although critical of the way the carnage has got politicised, they always remember with gratitude those who helped save their lives in that moment of terror.

Kashmir's is an inspiring story of courage. The president of the Riot Victims Welfare Society in Mohali and a member of the general council of Akali Dal Badal in 2009, this strong woman of fifty-seven, who makes it a point to be at the forefront of political rallies and protests in Mohali city, breaks down while recounting the massacre she witnessed in her trans-Yamuna colony of Bhajanpura in Delhi in 1984. She, like Lakhbir, is indebted to her neighbours. "We will be ever grateful to our Hindu neighbours who helped save our lives. My husband, Pritam Singh, along with others, was hidden in a locked room and the women sat on the terrace with stones and red chilli powder. My twelve-year-old son's hair was tied into two plaits and a neighbour lent her daughter's frock for him to wear," she recalled.

When the mobs threatened to burn down the neighbour's house, Kashmir's husband, Pritam, came out of hiding. They decided to gather as many Sikhs from the neigbourhood as possible, pile them into trucks, and move them to a safer place. "We managed to reach the Nanaksar gurdwara by the Yamuna bridge even though three attempts to attack us were made en route. We survived, but those who could not get into the trucks were killed," she said. Later, following instructions from the gurudwara, Pritam went back to Bhajanpura to round up orphaned children. He had to make his way through the burnt bodies of the neighbours to do this. He also saw that their house had been completely ransacked. "The shock was so great for my husband that when he returned, he suffered a stroke. Since then he has remained in poor health," Kashmir revealed.

All that Kashmir and Pritam found remaining in their home was a bed which they loaded onto a truck and then headed for Ludhiana, to be with relatives. But that arrangement did not work out in the long term. So they moved to a gurudwara in Chandigarh's Sector 15 from where social workers helped them secure a one-bedroom low-income group flat of the Punjab Urban Development Authority (PUDA) in Mohali. "I sold the bed for Rs 150, bought a stove and few provisions, and moved here," she said.

In the months that followed the anti-Sikh riots, there was a steady stream of families that came into different cities of Punjab to find refuge. Recalled Tejinder Singh Shergill, who was chairman of Mohali's Riot Victims Welfare Society in 2009: "Settling them here was not easy. PUDA and the government would regularly send eviction orders. But my uncle, Arjun Singh Shergill, and other social workers saw to it that these people were rehabilitated. As many as 704 homes were allotted to riot victims."

A visit to this colony, now called the Riot Victims Colony in Mohali's Phase XI, presents the picture of a ghetto of sorts, where many are still struggling to survive. This is also where Ravindar Kaur has made a home for herself. The daughter of a sevadar (employee) in Bala Sahib gurdwara near Ashram in Delhi, she had been married for six months when the riots broke out. "My husband and I had come to my parents' home. I had stayed home but my parents and husband had gone to attend a party and they were killed," Ravindar said.

Her husband's family, holding her responsible for the death of their son, turned her out. Later, she got married to Amarjit Singh, who had lost his wife and son to the violence. Today, Amarjit is over seventy years old and jobless. The couple has a married daughter and son, who is a special-needs child. Although poor, Ravindar is respected in the colony, as she is an active volunteer in the local gurdwara. "The old age pension of the government may not have reached us but the people have always come to our aid," she said.

Added Kashmir, "Some political elements try to inflame sentiments of the people but we try and pacify them. The Society follows up the cases of genuine victims and helps those living below the poverty line." But, according to her, doing this has not always been easy and there have been instances where actual victims never got compensation, while fake ones managed to get flats.

Apart from actively working for the riot-hit, many faceless women have also played the role of caregivers for those rendered physically disabled by the riots. After being bed-ridden for the past twenty-five years, Gurcharan Singh, 42, passed away in February 2009, in Balongi village near Chandigarh. He had been thrown into a burning vehicle outside his house in Delhi's Nawada colony during the riots. He never got any compensation and it was his elder brother's wife who looked after him. On March 11, 2008, he found the strength to depose before the Central Bureau of Investigation, revealing that a prominent Congress leader was with the crowds, inciting people to wipe out the Sikhs.

Commented Kashmir in conclusion, "We are deeply hurt by the fact that those who fomented those killings have not yet been punished. We got no justice and little or no compensation from the government. However, we continue to have faith in humanity because of the kindness that people from different communities, whether Muslim or Hindu or Sikh, demonstrated towards us."

Lessons from Gujarat: To Prevent Riots, Talk to Children

Deepti Priya Mehrotra

Ahmedabad (Gujarat): In 2002, Gujarat was the site of one of the worst communal riots in India's history, with tensions between Hindus and Muslims continuing to simmer long after the immediate violence had died down. The complicity of the state in the violence and the systematic hate campaigns against the minority community was so blatant that commentators often use the term 'pogrom' to describe the events of those stormy days. What made things even worse was the fact that many of those at the receiving end of the violence were from the poorest sections of society.

It was against this dark backdrop that Samerth, an Ahmedabad-based NGO, tried to make a difference. Founded in the early Nineties to promote participatory development among marginalised and vulnerable communities, it was one of the several organisations in the state that diligently worked towards bringing about reconciliation and peace in the post-riot atmosphere of distrust and disquiet.

Samerth founder-trustee Gazala Paul, a post-graduate in Coexistence and Conflict Management from Brandeis University (USA) said, in 2009, "In rural Kachchh, our main thrust was on sustainable livelihood practices, while in urban Ahmedabad our focus was on conflict resolution, peace-building and education. We got involved extensively in bastis (slums) through educational interventions for children and youth and livelihood restoration for women."

Working towards the economic restoration of riot-affected communities since 2003 in the Juhapura, Sarkhej, Jivraj, and Vejalpur areas of Ahmedabad – for the benefit of both Hindus and Muslims in the area – Samerth found that the memory of the 2002 violence still troubled people. Most of them were impoverished, largely because of the inadequate compensation given to them by the government in the aftermath of the violence and because of poor civic facilities, generally.

The organisation, therefore, sensitively developed interventions to help overcome the deprivation even as it attempted to change entrenched attitudes of prejudice and hatred. Realising that Self-Help Groups (SHGs) in the shanty towns of the city could provide a vital entry point to mobilise women of both communities, Samerth activists enabled SHG members to set up a savings and credit system as a means of supplementing their incomes. They also made loans available to riot-affected families.

The encouraging response from women of both Hindu and

Muslim communities initiated a process of rebuilding trust between them and greater integration. But the most important initiative Samerth launched was focused on children. It sought to make an impact on young minds by developing out-of-the-box approaches – especially by devising peace modules to tackle the effects of violence.

Shortly after the riots, it ran playgroups in the relief camps. "At that point," recalled Iqbal Baig, the organisation's programme support coordinator, "our focus was more therapeutic in nature. After the closure of the camps, we shifted the pre-schools within the communities to provide pre-school education and carry out peace education with schoolchildren, youth and adolescents, community leaders and the clergy."

A few thousand children – with a fair representation from both the Hindu and Muslim communities – actively participated in the 'peace classes' held in neighbourhood government and private schools in Ahmedabad. The peace modules tackled common biases and brought about a feeling of goodwill and mutual understanding. Quizzes and games, stories about eminent national leaders, special exercises such as the 'spider web' and the 'tree exercise', all helped children focus on topics of peace, non-violence, unity in diversity and social harmony, in a creative and fun way.

Fatma Chopra, a Samerth field worker, who had been actively engaged in developing the peace modules as well as in teaching and conducting classes for young children, explained, "Through our peace modules and quiz competitions, we tried to develop respect and tolerance in the minds of children from different religious and cultural backgrounds. By 2007, we were conducting peace modules in thirty-seven schools. Children got very interested in the approach and there were animated debates on diversity and multiculturalism."

But there were challenges too, as Nasrin Pathan, a peace educator, candidly admitted, "Initially, schools were hesitant and refused permission. But we started inviting eminent personalities as observers. This helped create an environment of trust among the managements. Slowly more schools agreed to cooperate with us."

Samerth then ran playgroups, exposing children to computers and other creative activities even as they got to understand the meaning and importance of multiculturalism. The organisation also encouraged schools to form Parent Teacher Associations as platforms to discuss issues related to harmony and peaceful coexistence.

Paul explained: "Gujarat had experienced a sequence of communal violence which left a deep impact on the hearts and minds of the people. As a result, the minority community members were forced to huddle together in different settlements like Juhapura, forming ghettoes. The lack of trust between people was so manifest that inter-community interactions had virtually stopped. This isolation allowed conservative and regressive elements to take control and curb reforms and progress. We worked in such an environment and often it was a huge challenge. To gain strength, we reached out to other organisations and built alliances to counter communal prejudices and tackle issues of injustice together. We made efforts to strengthen our networks for wider reach and impact."

The organisation specialised in providing training sessions on conflict transformation and peace-building. It built alliances with bodies such as the Ahmedabad Women's Action Group, Sanchetana, and the Self-Employed Women's Association, which had already set up SHGs among riot-affected communities.

In order to dispel divisive myths and stereotypes, Samerth widely disseminated amongst children, teachers and parents, the Gujarati translation of a study on multicultural traditions that it had conducted in association with the Tata Institute of Social Sciences. Entitled *Gujarat Unknown - A Study on Syncretic Traditions*, the study traced the multicultural traditions of the state through shrines, anecdotes and experiences, and observed that communities in this region had coexisted for centuries and carried out livelihood activities together, particularly in rural areas. These booklets proved effective in building a general appreciation of how cultures everywhere, including in Gujarat, have influenced each other and how reinforcing diversity is a precondition for human existence and an effective democracy.

As Paul said, "It took enormous energy and hard work on the part of Samerth staff to convince the schools, youth and women living in the slums to allow us to dwell upon issues of communalism, secularism and peace. But the processes of reconciliation are well-established and we are very happy when we see children responding to our work." Rehana Sheikh, a peace module teacher, added, "When we went into schools we had worked with in the Vejalpur, Jivraj and Sarkhej areas, the children there were friendly and talkative. They shared stories of violence and displayed a genuine interest in other religions and customs. Some of them had even become torch-bearers of the movement against communal feeling."

Samerth's is just one modest example of how a transformation of attitudes, even in the most challenging of circumstances, can be achieved with some innovative conceptualisation. In a climate of communal tension and distrust, the most important site of change is that of the mind of a child. Adding value to concepts like secularism and diversity can go some way towards ensuring that the tragic events of 2002 are never repeated in the Gujarat of the future.

Assam's Women Writers Capture Conflict's Many Shades

Uddipana Goswami

Guwahati (Assam): Incidents of rape by security personnel are not unheard of in Assam, where insurgent violence and ethnic conflict have raged for decades. There was, for instance, the October 2008 case involving two Central Reserve Police Force personnel, who were accused of raping two women in Udalguri district, which falls under the Bodoland Autonomous Territorial Districts. They were later exonerated. This led to various protests, including those led by Anjali Daimary, a littérateur and president of the Bodo Women's Justice Forum. In an act reminiscent of the action of the Meira Paibis in Imphal (Manipur) in 2004, Daimary and a group of peasant women came out on the streets of Rowta Chariali with the words 'Rape Us' inscribed on their chests and backs.

Indeed, women have been at the forefront of the Bodo struggle for political self-determination. The Bodos, despite being the largest indigenous community in Assam, have long felt dominated by the Axamiya-speaking Hindu community at the helm of all cultural, political and socio-economic power in the state. Their resentment against this domination often found expression in different political protests. By 1987, a full-scale mass movement was launched for a separate state of Bodoland, with the All Bodo Students Union (ABSU) taking the lead.

What started as a peaceful non-violent struggle soon turned violent in some pockets, with ABSU floating a military wing: the ABSU Volunteer Force. Women also participated in some measure – although never as direct combatants – in the violent activities that gradually grew in intensity with the emergence of more armed militant formations, like the Bodoland Liberation Tigers (BLT). In 2003, after the Bodoland Territorial Council (BTC) accord was signed, four contiguous districts – Kokrajhar, Baska, Udalguri, and Chirang – came under BTC jurisdiction. But even BTC control did not put an end to the cycle of violence in the region. Fratricidal killings continued, with a handful of the ethnic elite gaining immense power, while the majority lower down in the social and economic order continued to live in deplorable conditions.

The years of blood clashes and the ever-present threat of violence found reflection in the writings of a few Bodo women who chose to use their pen to describe the realities of their times. Renu Bodo, the first Bodo woman postgraduate in the state, has long been endeavouring to create a forum for all Bodo women writers in order to gather together their dispersed voices so that they can be heard.

Renu, who has written extensively on social and cultural issues, said that although her literary works were not exclusively on subjects relating to the Bodos, they did aim at raising social consciousness and cultural pride within the community. She hoped that her work would "inspire us to look within and identify our shortcomings, instead of blaming those around".

Pramila Narzary is another Bodo woman writer who has, in her fiction, criticised the violence and corruption that persisted in the region. In 2005, she became the first Assamese writer/translator to win one of India's highest literary awards – the Sahitya Akademi award – for her translations in the Bodo language, after it was granted recognition under the Eighth Schedule of the Indian Constitution in 2003.

Her short story "NREGA Jagra Hagra", for instance, was about how political and community leaders have deprived the common people of their dues under state-sponsored schemes for rural development, like the Mahatma Gandhi National Rural Employment Guarantee Act, which guarantees 100 days of wage employment to certain rural households. The story carries a message of hope as, in the end, ordinary people rise up against rampant corruption. Although "NREGA Jagra Hagra" upheld the importance of political protest, Pramila maintained that subjects like conflict are incidental to her writing.

But there are not many women like Renu and Pramila. Although the Bodos have been engaged in a nearly two-decade-long (1987-2003) conflict with the State, not many have directly addressed the issues of insurgent violence and the politics of identity, separatism and sovereignty in their work. As Renu said, "We would, at the request of our leader, write one-act plays or poetry with political messages during the years that the Bodo movement was going on, so that they could be performed in rallies and political meetings. They might have been printed in souvenirs or journals, thereafter, but we have not compiled them." This is indeed a sad commentary on the political literature of Assam. Not only is it occasional, it is undervalued – that is, where it exists at all.

Consciously political writers – whether women or men – are a rarity not just among the Bodos, but also in Assam in general. Very few writers have dealt with contemporary political realities and even fewer have used literature for protest. Given the highly charged political atmosphere that has marked the state for so many years, it is surprising to note that just a few writers have used a potent tool like literature to get their political messages across. Political activist Anjali Daimary, for instance, has led hundreds of women in public protests, but as a translator who has also won the Sahitya Akademi award for translation in 2007, her literary pursuits have not been overtly political.

There are some exceptions, of course. Anju Daimary, a writer who lives in Kokrajhar, claimed that while she is not a consciously political writer, she does recall conceiving a satire in verse on the "corpse of democracy" after witnessing the many irregularities in the first democratic elections to the BTC. These elections were held in 2006, three years after the signing of the BTC accord, and they were characterised by a mad scramble for power, which led to immediate factionalism among the accord's signatories as well as the creation of various disempowered sections – including women – within the community who did not get any representation on the council.

Anju happens to be one of the very few Bodo writers who has focused on the human aspects of the protracted armed conflict in the region that has also led to the dehumanisation of some sections of the community. One of her short stories, "The Test", deals indirectly with insurgent violence. Its protagonist, a trainee militant, debates questions of mindless killings. Ordered to assassinate an innocent old man, the trainee feels "sweat on my forehead. When I set my target on birds, cats or dogs, I didn't have to battle with my feelings.

Now I felt my hands heavy, as if all the weight of my whole body had gathered in my right arm." In the end the task is done. "Dumbly now, I followed the lieutenant across the river. I couldn't turn my head back. The bright moon was shining as a witness over my head." Anju's words create a powerful image of the human response to the conflict and moral struggles that it entails.

In writers like Anju and Pramila lies the hope that there will be others like them who will – whether consciously or not – capture the impacts of conflict and violence on ordinary lives.

The Power of One

"I felt resilient because I knew instinctively that I was on the right path."

Maoist Violence is not Prabhavati's Way

Manisha Prakash

Jehanabad (Bihar): Peering into the classroom of the anganwadi centre in Bhitiyan village, in Bihar's Jehanabad district, we could see a motherly figure giving instructions to her students. "Jump children. It helps in the development of muscles," she was saying. The children followed her instructions, bobbing up and down in neat rows. After the exercise, she asked them to sit down and recite a poem. Within minutes, the small classroom echoed with young, sing-song voices reciting, "Machchli jal ki rani hai..." (the fish is the queen of the water...), a popular Hindi rhyme. Then regular class work began.

This was in 2009, when we visited Prabhavati Devi, who was in her mid-fifties. What struck us immediately was the manner in which she related to her students and how she could awaken curiosity in their young minds. Later, as lunch time came and the bell rang, the children rushed out to grab their plates and line up to be served a generous portion of their midday meal of khichdi (a preparation of rice and lentils). Their alert teacher made sure that no child was left out.

Day after day, this was Prabhavati's routine. At first glance, her simplicity was obvious and there was nothing particularly unusual about her other than the fact that she ran the anganwadi at Bhitiyan meticulously. Yet, Prabhavati, who spoke only the local dialect, Magahi, turned out to be nothing like the ordinary village woman she appeared. Hers, in fact, was a rather extraordinary life.

In 1971, at the age of seventeen, Prabhavati got married to a man who had a different approach to life: he was not bothered about mundane things like raising a family, but was engaged in a 'struggle of the oppressed' that often involved killing innocent people. He was a Maoist. So, whereas the average newly married woman around here chiefly spent her time running her household, Prabhavati's early days as a young bride involved running away from the police. When we met her in 2009, Prabhavati was living alone in her brother-in-law's house in Shukulchak village. After living in fear and uncertainty for years, she had left her husband's home, which was located not too far away, because the police would regularly come and ransack it on the pretext of looking for him.

Although Prabhavati was all alone now, she felt that her life had a purpose. "I am fighting against ignorance by lighting lives with education and seeing to it that the poor get their due," she said with a deep sense of satisfaction. Her efforts in this regard hadn't gone unrewarded: in August 2008, she was named the Aadarsh Anganwadi Sevika (ideal anganwadi worker) of her village and the then Jehanabad District Magistrate Sanjay Kumar Agraval presented her with a certificate for exemplary service.

When asked whether she missed her husband – the erstwhile chief of the Naxalite outfit, People's War Group, in Bihar and later a central committee member of the banned Communist Party of India (Maoist), the dreaded Dev Kumar Singh alias Arvind Kumar alias Vikas – her reply was terse and quick: "I know what the future holds. He may be gunned down or jailed some day. I have accepted life the way it is."

There is a long list of crimes attached to Dev Kumar Singh's name. He is an accused in over twenty-five cases of violence and the alleged killings of several feudal lords and police personnel, including the assassination of eight Central Reserve Police Force jawans (soldiers) in a landmine blast in the Masaurhi subdivision of rural Patna in 1999. Moreover, it has been said that he has admitted to the killing of a deputy superintendent of police and five policemen at Dhanarua in 2001, besides blasting the Nadaul railway station, and looting seventeen rifles after killing a hawaldar (constable) of Bara police picket under Naubatpur police station. He is also believed to be one of the Maoists behind the audacious Jehanabad jailbreak of November 13, 2005, that resulted in the escape of over 200 Maoists who had been incarcerated in the Jehanabad sub-jail.

In sharp contrast to her husband, the very sight of arms and ammunition was disturbing to Prabhavati. She stated in quiet tones, "I am contributing to the uplift of society too, but mine is a peaceful way. Of course, if someone tries to violate my rights, I will raise my voice as I have always done. I am not someone to be cowed down."

Fondly called netayeenji (woman leader), Prabhavati came across as a well-respected village member and she was much sought after when it came to naming newborn babies. "Our children go to her centre to take lessons. She loves them like her own," said Reema Devi, a resident of Bhitiyan village, who was not in any way scared or intimidated by the fact that Prabhavati was the wife of a Naxal leader on the run. Added another local woman, Manjhilal Thakur, "Children like to be around her. No one has any problem with her. In fact, we have great regard for her. We are not even scared of her husband."

A graduate of D.N. College, Masaurhi, Prabhavati was appointed anganwadi sevika in 1991, and worked hard as a teacher for over two decades to earn the gratitude and love of everyone in Bhitiyan. Initially, however, life for her and her children had not been so simple. The family came up against many a trial, social as well as financial. Her father-in-law, a head clerk with the Public Works Department, had tried to persuade her husband, a physics graduate, to take up a job, but he refused. Although he tried working in a cooperative bank for seven months, dissatisfied, he soon traded in his status as a banker for that of a Maoist activist.

In his absence, Prabhavati raised her two sons and a daughter with the support of her in-laws. And her children followed in her footsteps. Her eldest son, Rakesh Ranjan, made teaching his profession and started a physics coaching centre in Patna, while daughter, Amrita, graduated from J.D. Women's College in Patna and got married. Her youngest son, Abhishek, studied engineering from the prestigious IIT

Kanpur and set up his own software company in Delhi. Eventually, both her sons married of their own choice and have settled down away from their home town. Although they tried to convince their mother to come and stay with them, Prabhavati opted to continue her work in the village and live off her meagre anganwadi wages and the additional income from her five bighas of land (one bigha equals 0.4 hectares).

Life may have dealt Prabhavati some harsh lessons, but she has no regrets. All she wanted to do was to serve the local people and to do so fearlessly. Summing up her general approach, she said, "If you are scared, people scare you. If you are not, they do not dare to."

Mother Courage: Turning Grief into a Search for Justice

Geeta Seshu

Mumbai (Maharashtra): "I know that my son will not return, but I want punishment for the culprits. I want justice from the government," said Akhtar Hasan Wagle, in a quiet but firm voice, as she sat by a grilled window that overlooked the spot where the police had shot her son, Shahnawaz, in an alley near Dockyard Road in south-central Mumbai.

Shahnawaz was only seventeen on January 10, 1993, when he was gunned down by the Byculla area police. He died a day later in hospital. But for the determination of his family not to remain mute and beaten, he would have been just another statistic of the second phase of violence that tore through Mumbai in 1992-93 in the wake of the demolition of the Babri Masjid.

Akhtar, in her early sixties, and her husband, Tahir, live with the slender hope that the overwhelming evidence before the authorities will stir them into taking action. During a visit to the couple's quiet home in 2009, Tahir remarked brokenly, "Even the report of Justice B.N. Srikrishna, who was appointed by the Maharashtra government to investigate the riots, has termed the death of my son 'cold-blooded murder' – paragraph 5.58 of the Srikrishna Commission Report. Surely, someone will listen to us."

In contrast to her husband, Akhtar displayed a calm and stoic demeanour. After she lost her older daughter, Arifa, in a drowning accident in Ratnagiri a decade ago, this brave mother's life revolved around Yasmin, her other daughter, and the family's fight for justice for Shahnawaz.

For the nearly two decades since the death of her son, Akhtar and her family have continued to live in the same small corner room on the second floor of Mumbai's Pathan chawl. The same room that overlooks the alley where his body once lay. Each day, Akhtar relives those moments. "It happened just here," she said, her voice shaking. Then, controlling herself, she continued, "The police came house to house and pulled out all the men, young and old. They pulled Shahnawaz from my hands and took him away. Before anyone could say anything, they had shot him. My daughter saw them from a crack in the window. She ran downstairs to him but they hit her with rifle butts and drove her back upstairs."

The mother and sisters watched as the police placed the youth's body onto a vehicle and took it to the city's J.J. Hospital. Tahir, to his eternal regret, was in Ratnagiri at that point. The family had gone there to visit a dargah (shrine) at Vishalgadh, and his wife, son, and daughters had chosen to return to Mumbai right after, despite reports of the outbreak of violence. It was only after Tahir returned four days later that the family could claim the body of their son. "I'm told he survived for a day in the hospital but no one could go to him. The city was under curfew and the women of my family could not venture out. They did not even tell me that he had been shot, they just told me to come back," Tahir recalled.

Despite the tragedy they are living through, the Wagles

firmly believe that their son did not die at the hands of Hindu groups or their Hindu neighbours, who lived in the adjoining Rustom Daruwala chawl. According to their painful reconstruction of the events of that fateful day, the police had acted on an anonymous complaint that bottles had been thrown by someone from Pathan chawl. "My son and his cousin, Arif, were daring and helpful boys. They braved the violence to get milk, bread, and food for the women stuck in their homes. I guess this was why they were targeted," Tahir surmised. While the police even dragged an eighty-five-year-old blind man out during that raid, Arif managed to escape by hiding under a bed in his home, as the women of his family sat on the mattress, almost suffocating him in the process.

Shahnawaz couldn't save himself. This despite the fact that his father was a well-known figure in the area, being very active in local social groups. In fact, Tahir was familiar to the local police as well. He owned a jeep that was, ironically, requisitioned by the police during the riots. "They came to our house and shouted to us to throw down the keys of the jeep. We told them it had no diesel but they said it didn't matter and took the vehicle," recalled Akhtar. The couple often wonders: perhaps if the police had known that the boy they had shot was Tahir Wagle's son, they may have given him better medical help and he might have survived.

But violence, in its madness, picks its victims without any reason. The policemen who shot Shahnawaz reportedly boasted that beneath their uniform they were Shiv Sainiks to the core, owning up to their sympathy with the local political party.

The Wagle family, on its part, has determinedly sought to secure justice against police officers K.L. Bishnoi, the then deputy commissioner of police of Zone III; Kishore Mankar, then senior inspector of Byculla police station; Ulhas Patankar, senior police inspector; Wahule and Balme, police inspectors; and Ramdesai and Gorasawant, police sub-inspectors. Their daughter, Yasmin, as an eyewitness, gave evidence before the Srikrishna Commission.

"We went for every hearing of the Commission. At first, Yasmin was very frightened, but I told her that whether she was afraid or not, she must go and give evidence. We went before the Commission with great hope," said Akhtar. Yasmin, older to Shahnawaz by only two years, was so shaken by his death that she didn't want to appear for her Class XII board examinations. But, once again, Akhtar recalled, wiping away her tears, "I told her: 'Your life is before you. You must study further. He won't return, but you have to make your life.'"

Later, the Commission, in its recommendations, sought action against those who were attached to the Byculla police station, naming Patankar, Wahule, and Ramdesai. The Commission's report stated that their conduct during the riots was extremely communal, that they had refused to record complaints in which Hindus were the accused, and that they had harassed and ill-treated Muslims. It further noted that their conduct indicated an attempt to shield miscreants belonging to Shiv Sena (C.R. No. 591 of 1992), and termed an "eyewash" the inquiry conducted by Surinder Kumar, a deputy commissioner of police, into Shahnawaz's death.

Together, Shahnawaz's family has tried to pick up the pieces of their lives. Yasmin got married in 1996 and moved to the Middle East, but she is committed to coming back to give further evidence if required. Every festival, birth, or death in their larger family, every report that a friend of Shahnawaz's has got a job, got married, or had a child, brings joy. But it brings sorrow, too, since it stirs the memory they carry of their son's hopes and dreams. "He was such a smart boy, so good at studies. He was studying in Elphinstone College and wanted to join the shipping line like his father and grandfather. He loved playing cricket," Akhtar whispered.

The Wagles tell whoever wishes to hear about their son's death that their hope is that Shahnawaz will get justice. For them, forgetting is not an option. Yet, Akhtar was puzzled when asked whether she ever felt angry at the death of her son and at the way politicians of all stripes sometimes stoke the fires of communal hatred. Her reply had a directness that was all the more poignant: "Yes, the politicians are responsible for communal violence. It is all a game for them. But I don't get involved in politics. I only want justice for my son, that's all."

A House for Nasreen, Riot-Affected

Shobha S.V.

Mumbai (Maharashtra): The riots that swept India's commercial capital, Mumbai, in 1992-93, had multi-dimensional impacts on the lives of their survivors. Some lost close family members and got caught up in an unending search for justice. Others lost family members as well as the property they owned, including their homes, and were left without a roof over their heads or a neighbourhood they could call their own.

Nasreen Bano, in her early forties, was a resident of a neighbourhood called Indira Nagar, which lay in the dense Mandala settlement of the Mumbai suburb of Mankhurd. During the riots, her family, along with several others, fled from home and took refuge in some cramped quarters in the heart of Mumbai's Byculla area, where the terrified residents formed themselves into squads to keep out potential attackers.

After the violence subsided, Nasreen's family moved into an abandoned mill in the neighbourhood of Madanpura, some kilometres away, along with many other Muslim families similarly displaced. Later, in 1999, when life seemed to have settled down a bit, Nasreen and her husband, a tailor by profession, purchased a small plot of land for Rs 14,000 in their old neighbourhood of Indira Nagar from a local slumlord and built a small house on it. However, the respite proved to be short-lived: a government-organised demolition drive in 2004 brought down what the state termed an illegal slum settlement.

Thereafter, Nasreen, along with her older family members and her two sons and two daughters, was forced to live on the streets. Eventually they, and some other homeless neighbours, moved back to Indira Nagar and constructed a makeshift shack on the same spot where their home had once stood. But once again, tragedy struck in 2006 as a fire destroyed all of Indira Nagar. Most of the inhabitants of the slum worked in the informal sector and they lost all their belongings, as well as their small livelihood ventures.

This pattern of dispossession, caused by circumstances ranging from communal riots to slum fires, has been fairly typical of the evolution of Indian cities like Mumbai. Explained Amita Bhide, an associate professor at the Tata Institute of Social Sciences, who has worked on urban displacement issues in Mumbai, "Women are the ones usually at home when demolitions take place. They go through immense pressure owing to the fear and unpredictability of a demolition. Besides, the onus of proving that her family is in 'legal' residence (as per the state government norms, which keep changing from time to time) puts extreme pressure on her. The feeling of being powerless, without having the strength of education and contacts in the right places, can wreck anybody. This intense pressure, followed by the need to carry on with life, can be a very heavy burden."

Interestingly, being witness to a series of unfortunate experiences that have each culminated in a state of homelessness, only sharpened Nasreen's sense of herself as a citizen with rights and strengthened her resolve not to be a victim. In 2008, rallying along with several women of her neighbourhood, she confronted the government over its policies involving slum dwellers and asserted her right to housing in the city. They joined the Ghar Bachao, Ghar Banao Andolan (Save a Home, Build a Home Movement).

That year, under the banner of the Andolan, Nasreen and others submitted a housing project proposal to the state housing department and the Central Urban Poverty Alleviation Ministry, which administers the government's Basic Service for Urban Poor scheme. For this rather unique proposal, the Andolan hired an architect to design building apartments on the fourteen-acre plot on which Indira Nagar stood, with a 269 sq ft house for each family. The proposal also envisaged a school, a primary health care centre, and a dispensary within the neighbourhood.

Said Nasreen, when we met her in 2009, "The government does not want jhopadpattis (shanties). So why don't they give us the authority to build homes? Why is it handing over the land to wealthy builders and developers for a pittance? Why can't they give the land to us? We have mazdoors (labourers) in our midst. All the government has to do is to give us the land and we will build our homes for ourselves. After all, we are the people who have built the houses in this city."

Andolan members met frequently to discuss the progress of their demands and their problems. While the government and major civil society organisations termed such dwellings 'encroachments', Nasreen emphatically refuted the claim. "These areas were plain quicksand. There was nothing here. We spent our hard-earned money, brought mud, and dumped it here to make the surface strong enough to build on. After we have done all the hard work, the government now wants to reclaim the land. Where was the government all this time? We surely have rights to this land," she said. She also pointed out that the people who lost their houses because of the demolition in Indira Nagar had valid voter ID cards.

The demands that Naseen and her friends were making were not without reason. After all, who doesn't want to live in a proper neighbourhood? Of course, Indira Nagar was far from ideal. Despite paying close to Rs 1,000 per month for their rented shanty, the families here did not have any water or sewage facilities and water-logging was a regular occurrence, especially during the rainy season. Moreover, during the monsoon, this area was a hotbed for epidemics. Nasreen acutally referred to the deluge that affected life in Mumbai in July 2005 as a "tsunami".

Meanwhile, the local community, on its part, was trying

hard to bring some semblance of stability to their turbulent, unsettled lives. Upon touring the neighbourhood in 2009, we saw a functional balwadi (nursery for children) filled with sketches and paintings of homes drawn by the children, poignantly reflecting their innermost desires. A mosque in one corner of Indira Nagar was the lone testament to the fact that there had existed a vibrant community here before the riots and demolition.

In many ways, Nasreen's family was still reeling under the tragedy of the communal riots that had stuck the city two decades ago. "My family was reduced to nothing after those riots. I lost my father and sister, and one of my brothers became mentally unstable," she recalled. The family was able to sustain itself largely on the earnings of a younger brother, an electrician. Nasreen's big worry was that her youngest sister, in her late twenties, had not yet been married. But they had no money to arrange a marriage for her.

Despite being a riot survivor, Nasreen was pragmatic enough to recognise that basic needs like housing know no communal divide. "Both Hindus and Muslims want their homes to be rebuilt and both communities are united on this," she pointed out.

She had made up her mind that whatever the future might bring, she would not relinquish her right to a home in Indira Nagar. "Why should we leave? This is our neighbourhood. I refuse to go anywhere else," she stated, clinging to the hope that the housing proposal put forward by the Ghar Bachao, Ghar Banao Andolan would be seriously considered by those who wield the levers of power in the city.

Will Nasreen's demand for a foothold in Mumbai be recognised? Only the future will tell.

Gujarat Riot Kids Come Home – To Faraway Delhi

Sukhmani Singh

Jamia Nagar (Delhi): Set against the grim statistics of the 2002 Gujarat pogrom, a saga of hope unfolded in the bylanes of Delhi's Muslim-dominated enclave of Jamia Nagar. Love and harmony was the predominant leitmotif in a nondescript three-storeyed building here, home to twenty-two slum children from Gujarat. For these children, aged six to seventeen, their ebullient warden, Asma Khan, 48, was mother, mentor, and guide, someone who was determined to prove that "there is nothing greater than the power of love".

Established in 2002 by a Muslim charitable organisation – the Zakat Foundation – to accommodate twenty-seven children who had been rescued from camps for riot-affected communities – twenty-two of whom were from Gujarat – the house later became the home of an equal number of children from the shanty towns of Uttar Pradesh and Bihar.

For Asma, who left a comfortable job as principal of an east Delhi school to work for these children seven days a week, caring became an all-consuming passion. Virtually nothing deterred her – neither the over one-hour-long commute from her home, leaving behind her own three children, nor the diverse challenges she tackled in a day's work. The lack of proper facilities was compensated for by her dedication as a caregiver. "Children have two sides to them, they can be moulded to become either good or bad. I have attempted to transform them through love and the right values," she remarked when we met her in 2009.

The children followed a rigorous daily schedule. Enrolled in an English-medium school in the vicinity, aptly called God's Grace, where donors paid 50 per cent of the fees, their evenings were meticulously divided into tuition time, an hour of religious instruction, and another to master the computer. Once a month a picnic was arranged as well.

As a smiling Asma bustled around, tasting the food, tidying the rooms, supervising homework, there were loud cries for "Asma aunty" coming from all corners of the building. There was a spat to be resolved, someone needed help with homework, another wanted a hand with a heavy bucket, while one child was just looking for a lap to cry on. As mother and peace-maker, she was near omnipresent.

Said Najma, 14, the eldest and brightest of three sisters brought here from a Gujarat relief camp in 2002, "Asma aunty has taught me what love is and how to solve the fights of the younger children with love. I have learnt to be firm in my beliefs, never to tell lies or harm anyone, always help others, be independent, and never lose sight of my goal." Her goal, she said, was to teach science, but her artistic talent had also blossomed, as evidenced by the pretty wall hangings she had made, innovatively crafted with empty egg trays and beads, which adorned the girls' dormitory.

While at least one parent of most of the children from the Gujarat relief camps had survived the pogrom, almost all had remarried or lived in such acute poverty that they did not have the means or ability to bring up their children with any degree of comfort. During their annual visits back home every summer, the children felt forlorn and unwanted. With their parents hard-pressed to give them a proper meal, they returned looking starved. As Najma tucked into her special Sunday lunch of biryani and stew, she shrugged and spoke of her recent visit home: "No one had the time for us back there and we felt lonely." Other children added, "We didn't feel happy when we went home. We missed Asma aunty very much."

Asma's love and dedication has also transformed previously traumatised boys into forward-looking and ambitious youngsters. Mohammed Farooq, 14, a wannabe cricketer, said, "When I first came here, I used to cry a lot. But Asma aunty solved all our problems. She treated us all equally and explained things to us." Added Wasim Akram, 16, who dreamt of becoming a doctor, "I never want to return to Gujarat, I feel insecure there. Coming here, I have truly understood the Qur'an. It teaches us to love everyone as our brothers. I don't know why Hindus and Muslims fight with each other." Nurtured in the peaceful environment of this home, where even toy pistols were taboo, most of these children had developed an overpowering desire to become successful and build schools and hospitals for Gujarat's poor.

But this journey from trauma to tranquillity was a long and arduous one. Asma recalled the hot summer day in 2002 when she first met the children, after officials of the Zakat Foundation arrived with them from Gujarat. "They were filthy, barefoot, some had defecated in their clothes, and they behaved like animals. The first thing the cook and I did was to scrub them down with a hose-pipe and shampoo," she recalled. Even though her husband was bedridden at that time and needed her attention, after meeting the kids Asma felt impelled to commit to making a difference to their lives. "As a devout Muslim, I feel that the most important thing in life is to help others. The children were in such a bad state I put aside my own needs for them," she said.

Mumtaz Najmi, joint secretary of the Zakat Foundation, was one of the team that brought the children to Delhi. "It was completely spontaneous. We chose those in the worst condition, fearing they would become extremists if they stayed on. They were so starved they would leap onto the food in the crowded relief camps," she said.

During their first few weeks in the city, the children were housed in two rooms in Okhla, a locality neighbouring Jamia Nagar. Bedding was hastily rented from a tent house and food was brought in from a hotel. Communication was a major problem, as the children spoke only their native Gujarati, so special Hindi classes were arranged for them in a central Delhi school. From washing bottoms and drying tears to stitching frocks for the girls, Asma spared no effort to give the children a sense of belonging. Gradually, the situation stabilised. A dry-fruit merchant from the Walled City in north Delhi lent them his home in Jamia to house the children and the Foundation later purchased it.

Asma recalled some of the worst moments from the past: "They would all gather together at dusk and start crying, as most of their homes had been burnt at night. One of them had stayed underwater all night to escape the rioters and suffered nightmares long after the incident. I would sit on the lawn with them till dawn, just hugging them."

Many of the boys also expressed their trauma through aggression, beating each other up in mindless violence. But Asma doggedly talked to them with love and compassion. Gradually, the children imbibed her own philosophy, which she said she had gleaned from the Qur'an: "Only people who lack humanity can hurt each other. No religion teaches you to fight or do ill to others. The world will become perfect only if you change yourself from within. It is your deeds that make you great."

Perhaps Asma was a product of her own experiences. Growing up in the north Indian city of Kanpur, she gave tuitions to pay for her graduation in political science, English, and Urdu from Delhi's Jamia Millia University. With a natural affinity for children, she worked as a nursery school teacher for two years before she got married. As the wife of a printing press proprietor in central Delhi's Daryaganj, her initial years of marriage passed by in a blur of peace and love, until her husband developed acute diabetes and fell seriously ill.

During his prolonged illness, which led to his early demise, the press her husband ran had to be sold and Asma became the family breadwinner. Financial travails forced her to shift her children from private to government schools, but they continued to perform well. She was of the opinion that everything worked out for her because she had dedicated her time and energy towards nurturing the underprivileged. With a smile, Asma concluded, "Ever since I took on their responsibility, my personal problems have ceased."

There's No Stopping Bimala's School

Ratna Bharali Talukdar

North Cachar Hills (Assam): When the Saron Lower Primary School in Saron village, Assam, was burnt down by extremists in an ethnic clash in 2003, Bimala Hmar, an assistant teacher there, took it upon herself to ensure that the education of the local children would not suffer at any cost.

Saron village, which is near Mahur, a small hill-station in the North Cachar Hills district, was attacked by suspected militants of the Dima Halam Daogah, an extremist group representing the dominant Dimasa tribe. Those were the days when there was a raging conflict between the Dimasas and the Hmars, another tribal community of the area, and the ensuing violence had resulted in the widespread displacement of people from both communities, with many innocents being killed in the process.

Nearly two-thirds of the houses in Hmar-dominated Saron were completely burnt down. The fire also consumed two lower primary schools and one high school. Everyone in the village had to take shelter in makeshift relief camps made of tarpaulin sheets and bamboo, located close to the Mahur police station and an army camp, about one kilometre away from their gutted homes.

Recalled Bimala, who was vice president of the Mahur unit of the Hmar Women's Association, when we met her in 2009, "Militants and miscreants attacked our village twice in 2003. The first attack was on April 9, when forty-eight houses were burnt down. In June, they came again, this time with more sophisticated arms and ammunition, and attacked Jeheron, one of the Hmar villages. When the police and security forces rushed to the spot, another group of miscreants entered our Saron village and set our homes and educational institutions on fire. The attack was so sudden and well-planned that we could not save anything."

Fortunately, Bimala's home, located in the third block of the village, escaped the devastating fire. So while others in the community were preoccupied with rebuilding their homes, Bimala concentrated on finding a way to ensure that the children of Saron would continue to get uninterrupted education. That was when she decided to run the school from her home. First, she discussed the idea with her husband, J. Malsown, who was working as a demonstrator at the local Department of Sericulture. He readily agreed to go along with her plan.

But it was a task easier said than done. Not only was their house too small to accommodate all the displaced schoolchildren, they also had no suitable school furniture. So Bimala decided to use her front yard and even converted a portion of the kitchen into a classroom for pre-primary children. "Textbooks and other study materials too had got destroyed. But we were determined to conduct classes and even hold examinations on schedule. As it turned out, although the children had to face displacement and hunger, they did not lose their academic year," smiled Bimala.

In time, the villagers realised that Bimala had not just restored education amidst violence, she had also initiated a process of rebuilding life amidst great devastation. Thanzual Khojor, a resident of Saron, put it this way: "Life was at its most hostile in relief camps. We had to spend days in acute hunger and penury and were afraid to return to our homes for fear of being attacked again. We were also extremely worried about the future of our children, their education and health. But we noticed that whenever they came back from Bimala Hmar's school, they had smiles on their faces. We then realised that we should not waste any more time fearing the future, but concentrate on trying to restore normalcy and peace by assisting Bimala and replicating her work."

In some of the most severely conflict-hit areas in Assam, including the Kokrajhar and Karbi Anglong districts, hundreds of thousands have been displaced and children have lost many years of schooling. In Kokrajhar district, for instance, some

3,14,000 people were displaced and had to live in relief camps for decades after a series of clashes between the Bodos and other tribal groups in the region in 1993, 1996 and 1998. Schooling in these relief camps began only in 1999 and, that too, at the government's initiative.

Bimala's makeshift school has been the only example of school education having been resumed immediately after a conflict situation in the state. What was even more noteworthy was that it was achieved at the initiative of a tribal woman. It actually encouraged Saron villagers to leave the relief camp as soon as they could and return home. Residents also collectively approached the administration and the Department of Education for rehabilitation as well as for the release of a grant to construct a school building. This community initiative worked out well and they were able to secure a financial grant of Rs 1,79,000 for a school in 2006.

As Bimala said, "The pain and agony of being displaced and losing our near and dear ones will haunt us forever. But by rebuilding our lives and by giving priority to education, we have been able to prove our resilience in the face of aggression and violence."

Her words were echoed by her students. Zonunthari Lungtau, who was in Class III at that time and then went on to study at the Presbyterian High School, the lone high school in the village, pointed out that it was Bimala who had taught her how to concentrate on studies, even in difficult situations. "Had she not guided us properly when we were in the relief camps, we would not have been able to continue our studies. I hope to become a doctor when I grow up," said the young girl.

Being a teacher and a woman of a minor hill tribe, Bimala made every effort to convey to the extremists that both the Hmars and Dimasas needed education and development, not conflict. That's because being one of four children of a village widow had taught her many lessons in life. "I had a tough life as a child. Even to buy books I had to work hard. After my matriculation, I could not go for higher studies despite my desire to do so, but managed to get the job of an assistant teacher. During the riots, I was a mute witness to the burning of our school, but I was determined to keep the dream of education alive in my students," stated this simple village woman endowed with both vision and courage.

Fighting for Prisoners' Rights, Clad in a Burqa

Arfa Khanum Sherwani

Hyderabad (Andhra Pradesh): The capital of Andhra Pradesh, Hyderabad, is known as a city of former nizams, historical monuments, centres of learning like the Osmania University, institutions of cyber technology – and for the infamous Mecca Masjid blasts of May 2007. Those blasts, which took place in a seventeenth century mosque, shattered the peace for which the city was renowned. Nine people were killed immediately and many more died later. They were to be followed a few months later by blasts at the Gokul Chat Bhandar and Lumbini Park.

Soon after the blasts, dozens of young men in the city were picked up by the police and charged with waging a war against the country. While the accused were in jails and their cases were being heard in courts, their families went through a harrowing time. Despite not being involved in any way with the blasts, they were considered tainted by their relationship with the accused. Several of them, including elderly parents and young children, faced social boycott, were thrown out of rented accommodation, and forced into a penurious existence. Even those inclined to help them stayed away for fear of a police backlash.

That was when Dr. Rafat Seema, 42, a teacher by profession with a doctoral degree, felt she had to step in to help the women in these families. Initially, she met with a lot of resistance and people advised her against involving herself in an issue that was so controversial. But Seema was determined to push ahead.

In 2008, along with Kaneez Fathima, a librarian by profession and a human rights activist, Seema set up the NISA Research and Resource Centre for Women. Although several women from almost all corners of Hyderabad and all walks of life came forward to support NISA's bid to help the affected families, the task at hand was not an easy one. It was not like doing charitable work to help the destitute. Most of the accused came from poor and marginalised families, with little economic or social clout. As for the women – wives, mothers, sisters – for the most part they were poorly educated and had few skills with which to make a living. The little assistance that did come their way was clearly inadequate. The situation demanded not just the rehabilitation of these families with some temporary financial help, but a long-term training programme that would give them the ability to actually earn an income in the absence of the family's breadwinners.

According to Seema, it was a complex situation and one that demanded a lot of time and commitment from everyone involved. Funds came in the form of individual contributions, while the work was done by volunteers – from PhD students at Osmania University to sympathetic housewives from local neighbourhoods. "We began by giving the affected women some money to buy sewing machines or open a shop or boutique. Setting up small enterprises and running them required training. Those who were educated were given jobs as teachers, tutors or social workers," said Seema, the general secretary of NISA, when we spoke to her in 2011.

Meanwhile, the imprisoned men faced long-drawn, tough legal battles. And every day they spent away from home meant no income for their families. Recalled one of the men who was later acquitted by the courts, "My world was completely devastated. Even my good friends were reluctant to talk to me. It was in such a situation that NISA extended a helping hand. If NISA hadn't been there as a source of support when I was in jail and after I was freed, I don't know what I would have done. I don't know what would have happened to my family. I owe a lot to this organisation." He added, "I only had to go to jail but it was my family which was really punished. They were alienated from the rest of the world. Only Seema baaji [elder sister] would go to my house and talk to the women, consoling them and helping them whenever possible."

Another young man, who was freed in 2008, was able to complete the final year of his Bachelor's degree in Unani medicine and surgery with NISA's support. He now runs a clinic as a qualified medical practitioner. When we talked to him, he revealed that Seema also helped him find his life partner. "No one wanted to marry a 'terrorist' like me, even though I had been proven innocent. Seema stepped in and helped me find a bride."

Seema added, "There is an entire life left to live. More than anything, what these unfortunate men need is human support and the assurance that they have people by their side."

Despite the hostile environment and repeated visits to the police station to face repetitive interrogation, the gutsy activist – who prefers to remain covered in a burqa from head to toe – remained undeterred. She knew that just showing sympathy for those jailed for terrorism could invite the charge that she was 'anti-national'. So how did she muster the courage to come out publicly in support of the prisoners? After all, NISA's initiative was the first of its kind in Hyderabad and there was really no way of confirming the innocence of the accused before the trial had run its course. Seema remembered the conundrum NISA faced: "Yes, there could have been a possible error in judgement. Just their arrests had made these men and, by association, their families 'traitors' in the eyes of the Hyderabadis. We did initially face a lot of roadblocks. The police would come and ask questions of us. I felt resilient because I knew instinctively that I was on the right path. In any case, I also knew that if they were, by any chance, convicted, even criminals and terrorists have some basic rights and those rights have to be protected in a democracy."

Seema also pointed out how the fundamental rights of women and children related to these men were violated during those days: "What was their crime? Can you imagine the suffering of the relatives of innocent men wrongly picked up by the police? Nobody is prepared even to listen to their side of the story!"

By 2011, many of those accused in the Mecca Masjid blasts had been pronounced innocent by the courts and their long months of suffering came to an end. Although it is impossible to make up for that lost time, life beckons them today, urging them to go ahead and achieve their full potential.

Observed Seema, "Their return to the mainstream is not a matter of a day or two, it is a process. It will take time. The best we can do for them in order to rehabilitate them fully is to trust them." Which is what she has done. In the process, she has also reminded the country that every human being has the right to dignity and justice.

In Gadchiroli's Zone of Fear, a Doctor Saves Lives

Shoma Sen

Gadchiroli (Maharashtra): Deep in the forests of Gadchiroli, a tribal district in eastern Maharashtra, live the Gond adivasis – among the poorest and most neglected people of the state. The region is considered dangerous because large parts of it have come under the sway of Maoist groups. The ensuing conflict between the militants and the State has turned the region into a zone of fear.

The forest is usually not a place where one would expect to find qualified doctors, especially ones who have studied at the world-renowned Johns Hopkins University in the U.S. But then, Dr. Rani Bang and her husband, Dr. Abhay Bang, who are both in their fifties and co-founders of the Society for

Education, Action and Research in Community Health (SEARCH), are not 'usual'.

Rani Bang (née Chari), the daughter of a doctor and granddaughter of a prominent Congress party member of parliament from Maharashtra's Chandrapur district, met Abhay, the son of the famous Gandhian, Thakurdas Bang of Wardha, at Nagpur's Government Medical College, where they were both studying. Abhay was also involved in the Sampoorna Kranti (Complete Revolution) movement initiated by political leader Jayaprakash Narayan. After their marriage, the couple went to Johns Hopkins to pursue higher studies. On their return, both Rani and Abhay, determined to take the road less travelled, resolved to place their powers of healing – as a gynaecologist and physician, respectively – at the service of government Primary Health Centres for the benefit of ordinary people.

In 1985, the couple set up SEARCH, a multipurpose village within a village. Located in Shodhgram, about fifteen kilometres from the district headquarters of Gadchiroli, on the Dhanora road, SEARCH is a hospital, a de-addiction centre, and a voluntary organisation that runs various projects on tribal welfare, health, adolescent sex education, and so on. It is also a research institute that has brought out many publications. Reminiscent of a tribal village, it is equipped with all the modern amenities necessary to meet its objectives. Mud houses amidst trees built around a common courtyard, hutments for in-house patients to live in with their families, a temple dedicated to Danteswari Devi, worshipped by the Gonds, and other symbols of tribal culture abound to make patients feel at home. "We asked the people what kind of a hospital they would like and then designed this facility," remarked Dr. Rani Bang, when we met her in 2009.

One of the greatest achievements of the SEARCH project has been to bring about a fall in the maternal mortality rate of the area through improved neonatal care. This has been done by introducing modern medicine and hygiene practices into the tribal lifestyle through camps, visits to villages, training of birth attendants and health workers from among the community, and by encouraging city-trained doctors to work in the area.

According to Sunanda, the women's health coordinator at SEARCH, maternal mortality has always been high in this region because childbirth is carried out at home in the most primitive way. "Earlier, women used to arrive at the hospital only in cases of an emergency, due to factors such as lack of transport, finances, and also a lack of faith in modern medicine. But this has changed gradually," she said. This positive behavioural change – including a growing preference for institutional deliveries – is largely because SEARCH workers have taken pains to explain the danger signs that pregnant women must watch out for so that they know when they must go to a hospital. "We explain about the anatomy, nutritious food, and convince the mothers-in-law to feed their daughters-in-law well," elaborated Sunanda, who has been associated with the project for fifteen years. Sunanda, originally from Nagpur, has done her Master's in sociology. She and her husband are both social workers employed by SEARCH.

Local customs are the reason for infant deaths, too. Traditionally, Gond mothers starve themselves for an easier birth, do not nurse for three days after their babies are born, and do not clothe the newborn for five weeks. As a result, pneumonia kills a large number of infants. In an attempt to address this concern, SEARCH has been encouraging mothers to check the weight of their newborns, among other measures. It has also trained traditional birth attendants, who could be any committed person who has attended to about four childbirths in the village.

Another SEARCH intervention has been in improving the condition of the traditional Gond korma – the rather dark and dirty hut in which women are isolated during menstruation. While it has been difficult to convince the community to do away with this practice of isolation altogether, SEARCH health workers have managed at least to improve the korma, turning it into a clean and comfortable place, with perhaps a bed and a tiled roof. The korma has, in fact, been transformed into a 'women's room', where they meet during their difficult days, rest, and share experiences.

Describing the SEARCH approach to improving the well-being of the Gonds, Sunanda spoke of the need to understand the essentials of Gond culture and build on their tribal heritage. "We don't laugh at the tribals, their beliefs or superstitions," she said, adding, "Their medicine is mainly herbal medicine and black magic practised by traditional healers. We tell the people that they should also take our modern medicine. We encourage them to bring their healer along and try to train him in modern medicine. Now the traditional healers trained by us carry malaria slides and give tablets."

At the other end of the spectrum, Dr. Rani Bang has been working on Gond tribal medicines, conducting scientific experiments to ascertain their efficacy. She has argued that the use of asafoetida to treat fungal infections of the skin, garlic for vaginal infections, and boiled guava leaves for anal fissures probably does have a sound scientific basis. Her book, *Goin* (a Gondi word for 'friend'), includes a study of the area's flora as seen through the eyes of Gond women and traditional healers. Her research has introduced her to a wealth of tribal knowledge and anecdotes. Yet, despite her wide exposure to tribal customs, there are times when she is left startled. Once, she was taken aback when a woman casually pointed to a plant that she claimed was useful to "kill a husband"!

But how can people work so selflessly in an area of conflict? Don't Rani Bang and her colleagues sometimes feel intimidated by their difficult circumstances? Said Rani, the 2008 recipient of the National Award for Women's Development through Application of Science and Technology, as well as many other national and international awards, "What is there to fear? After all, everybody has to die some day."

A Sri Lankan Tamil Refugee Builds New Worlds

Papri Sri Raman

Chennai (Tamil Nadu): V. Thenmozhi, in her late thirties, would have liked to have a life of her own – set up a home, build a career, become a mother, perhaps. Yet, all her plans have been put on hold for some time. "It is true that everyone wants to settle down, but for the moment my life revolves around the refugees from my country," she told us in 2009.

Thenmozhi wasn't exaggerating when she said that her life was dedicated to Sri Lankan Tamil refugees. This activist and counsellor has spent nearly two decades working with those who fled in the thousands across the Palk Strait to the Indian mainland, after the Sinhala-Tamil ethnic conflict broke out in the island nation in the early 1980s.

In 1990, Thenmozhi, then only a teenager, had to leave her village of Velanai in the Jaffna district of Sri Lanka, with her parents and a four-year-old sibling. Their destination was Madras (now renamed Chennai), where her elder brother and sister were already studying. Hers was a family of modest means, so they decided to reach Tamil Nadu on boat. That maiden voyage over choppy seas forced the young girl to reflect on her identity as an individual. "That dangerous trip made me wonder about who I was, about what the words 'my country' and 'my people' actually mean," she recalled. She had grown up hearing these words but had not really thought about what they signified. It was only the experience of being a refugee that made her realise their true meaning. Said Thenmozhi, "I kept thinking about my village, my land, and the friends I had left behind. I thought about all my people who were fleeing from their own country, day after day."

The Madras of those days was crowded with Tamil refugees. The Organisation for Eelam Refugees Rehabilitation (OfERR), set up in 1983, lent her family a helping hand in settling down. "I was brought to the OfERR office. Everyone who worked for rehabilitation here was a refugee and instantly I felt I was among my people," she said.

Thenmozhi, who had just completed Class X, went on to join a city college, but the unsettled conditions made it impossible for her to concentrate on her studies. Her father fell ill at that point – the experience of abandoning his homeland had been hard on him. There was also very little money in the family. All these factors made Thenmozhi decide to give up college and work for OfERR instead.

For the young Thenmozhi, the decision to work with OfERR was not just about taking up any job. How was an eighteen-year-old to counsel an eighty-year-old refugee? How was a young girl to advise a mother who had lost all her children while attempting to flee her village in a leaking boat? What Thenmozhi realised immediately was that she needed to be better equipped to understand people's tragedies and ease their apprehensions.

So she went through the leadership training programme that is compulsory for every counsellor and community worker at OfERR. Elaborating on this training, OfERR chief, S.C. Chandrahasan, explained, "Here they are taught how to be different from all the other refugees, how to think positively, how to look at ways to move on in life. A refugee's life is always in danger of stagnating."

By 1994, Thenmozhi had become a full-fledged counsellor. As part of her work, she had to go from camp to camp – there were 117 camps in Tamil Nadu – talking to angry destitute men, disconsolate women, and confused children who did not understand what had happened to them. "I had to first make friends with every group I met and then gain their confidence. This does not happen with just one meeting. So I had to go back again and again. Slowly, each one came out with his or her story. Their stories were all of loss and devastation," she said.

As she put it, over the next five years, the young woman learnt to be the tree that gave Sri Lankan refugees some shade, so that they could regain their strength and confidence to begin their lives anew. She also learnt typing and record-keeping, besides getting acquainted with issues like women's empowerment, gender equality, and family violence.

By 2006, Thenmozhi had acquired a diploma in social service management from Chennai's Loyola College. Not only did she gain new knowledge as she went along, she also shared it with others in the camps. She talked to them about how to initiate income-generating activities like setting up small shops, tailoring clothes, making baskets, and selling vegetables and fish.

In the course of these meetings and conversations, many heart-rending experiences came to be etched on her mind. She remembered, for instance, a very shy mother of three, who she met at the Toppukkollai camp in Pudukottai district in 1993-94. The woman had become a recluse: she had refused to speak to anyone in the camp for months and wouldn't even come out of her hut. It was to reach out to such women that OfERR decided to set up the Mothers' Sangam, an organisation of mothers that functioned within the refugee camps throughout the 1990s. Eventually, that reclusive woman who spoke to no one started going out of her home and, later, counselling others.

For Thenmozhi, the most satisfying part of her work lay in empowering women. Chandrahasan understood why this was the case. As he said, "For generations, women in this region have suffered a lot of injustice. The time has come to right the wrongs done to them. We, therefore, focus on women as builders of a new and aspiring generation. Our women refugees, their daughters and granddaughters – now there are three generations of Lankan Tamil women in Tamil Nadu – are our assets, our best human capital."

As elsewhere in the region, even among Lankan Tamils, traditionally it was the husband who went out to work. Becoming refugees meant that familiar patterns of life were altered completely. Explained Thenmozhi, "Women in the camps had to be a part of the income-generating process. But this was not an easy task. We had to teach them to assert themselves step by step: 'First, send your children to school. Start working. Learn to do small businesses. Join self-help groups. Set up small shops. Start vending something.' That's what we told them."

Her decades-long struggle has had its share of small satisfactions. She has witnessed love bloom and relationships develop in these camps. Once, a young refugee woman in the Thiruvathavur camp fell in love with a man, a painter, from outside the camp. They were soon married. One day, while working, the husband fell from a high platform and broke his back. He became disabled and lost his job. "We taught that woman how to make flower garlands. She began selling garlands in the camp itself [Tamil women generally wear jasmine flowers in their hair every day]. Soon, she taught her husband the work and he started making garlands while she sold them and they made a good living out of this activity," the veteran counsellor recalled, pride and affection writ large on her face.

Thenmozhi's stories span across 117 camps. It is a lifetime of work. She has also made sure that younger women have been trained to become inheritors of this struggle for empowerment. "So much blood has been shed because of this conflict, so much tragedy and repression have occurred. But we still have a collective dream of going home one day. If I have accomplished anything, it is to help create the feeling in our community that we have the strength to rise up from the ashes and take charge of our lives once again."

Kavita Karkare's Courage Quotient

Geeta Seshu

Mumbai (Maharashtra): The digital photo frame unit sat oddly on a mantelpiece stacked with medals and citations, including an Ashok Chakra awarded posthumously to Hemant Karkare in the wake of the November 26, 2008 attacks in Mumbai.

Full of photographs of the Anti-Terrorist Squad (ATS) chief in happy times, lovingly chosen by his daughter and set to his favourite Hindi film songs, the photo display vainly tried to drown out what became one of the many defining images of that Wednesday night: the ATS chief donning a bullet-proof jacket and helmet, only to be shot dead later.

After receiving news that Mumbai was under a coordinated shooting and bomb attack by terrorists, later identified as having originated from Pakistan and arrived via sea, the ATS chief rushed to his official vehicle and was proceeding along Mumbai's Rang Bhavan Road with additional commissioner Ashok Kamte, senior inspector Vijay Salaskar, and four constables, when the police party was fired upon by two of the attackers. Only one constable, Arun Jadhav, survived.

Along with scores of others who were glued to their television screens that night, Kavita Karkare also saw that last visual of her husband. Only a few hours earlier he had been eating dinner with his family at home.

Recalled Kavita, when we met her in 2009, a few months after those cataclysmic events, "Arun Jadhav came to meet me afterwards. He was very shattered. He told me how it had happened. But it took me at least two to three months before I could muster up the courage to visit the site of my husband's assassination near Cama Hospital. I wanted to see how it had happened and where; my sister-in-law was with me and we tried to picture it together."

For her, as well as for the other victims, the disconnect between the reality of their own shock, confusion, and grief and the events being played out on TV screens almost in real time was nearly impossible to come to terms with. Yet, barely a month after the death of her husband, Kavita had resumed duty as a lecturer in educational sociology in a Mumbai college, in order to finish the syllabus set for the students and prepare them for their forthcoming examinations. "I don't know how I did it, but I had to go back and finish my work," she recalled in a matter-of-fact tone that belied the effort it must have taken. Grateful that her students had respected her privacy and refrained from referring to her husband's death, she was pragmatic about the civil society response. She observed that many organisations had, in the aftermath of November 26, held meetings on the concerns the attack had raised, but while some were genuine, others were merely interested in projecting their own agendas.

Kavita believed her husband had made the ultimate sacrifice for his country. As she said, "He was that kind of person. One doesn't become a martyr suddenly; values of patriotism cannot be imbibed instantly. It was part of his childhood and growing up years. His parents played an important part in shaping his value system."

Hemant Karkare's father, Kamlakar Karkare, was a well-known communist in Nagpur, while his mother came from a family close to the Rashtriya Swayamsevak Sangh. Despite this marriage of people from opposing ideologies, the relationship was free of conflict. Karkare's parents, in fact, encouraged independent thinking and the roots of liberalism ran deep. Karkare's mother completed her education after her marriage, and even Kavita was encouraged to take up a job and complete a Bachelor's degree in education after she had married Hemant. "I worked in a bank earlier, but since I always loved teaching, I fulfilled my dream of doing a Master's in education as well. But I believe we need a revolution in the educational field, too. As teachers, we need to discuss and debate contentious issues with our students so that they can contribute to building a more aware society," she said.

For Kavita, November 26, 2008, was a defining day. She could not keep the disappointment from creeping into her voice when she said, "Some officers and politicians measured up, others didn't. Today's politicians fall short in their sense of patriotism. Where are people like Bhagat Singh in the country today?" Despite her calm and reflective demeanour, Kavita was bitter about the fact that officers like her husband had been sent into the field with little information, no reinforcements and, significantly, with poor equipment. "I am angry. This system has to be changed from within. There must be more transparency, politicians must be made accountable. If they do not perform, they must be removed," she declared.

In its report, the Pradhan Committee, appointed by the Maharashtra government to enquire into the incidents of November 26, virtually exonerated the police establishment. But this was at variance with the accounts that Kavita and Vinita Kamte, the wife of Ashok Kamte, who was also killed that night, managed to piece together. And although Kavita has never hesitated to publicly voice her criticism of the way the attack on Mumbai was handled, she has little hope of ever being heard by the decision-makers or getting any real justice for her husband and his colleagues.

Sitting in the living room of the official quarters she had permission to reside in for three more years, Kavita pointed to the driftwood lampshades, a wall clock, and a coffee table: all designed by her husband during his stint as superintendent of police in the Maoist-prone areas of Chandrapur district in eastern Maharashtra, a situation he had tried to read about and understand. The rest of the house was also full of souvenirs and mementos. Kavita recalled how her husband took a personal interest in home décor, rearranging the furniture and artefacts every fortnight. She also talked about his other interests, which ranged from listening to old Hindi film songs and Marathi abhangs (devotional songs), to reading books, especially those on philosophy and science. Her grief, as she remembered the good times spent with her husband, was writ large on her face.

While the events of the night attack that shook Mumbai may have begun to fade from public memory over time, its victims are still haunted by their trauma and loss. Kavita's two children, a son and daughter, have been her biggest support post-November 26, but she admitted that the family often felt isolated and that Hemant's assassination had created a permanent vacuum in their lives. Kavita pointed out that all those who had been affected by that attack were in need of assistance in some form or the other, and that monetary compensation alone was simply not enough. She made it a point to keep meeting the families of the other victims informally and talking to them. "They need help at every stage in their lives and there is no infrastructure or a social support system for them," she observed.

"Everyone says women are more courageous than men, but that is simply not true, going by my case. It's just perhaps that women are better survivors. Now I believe it is the responsibility of India's citizens to come forward and ask the important questions about November 26, 2008," concluded this woman who has come to embody courage in situations of conflict for many in India.